Choose Your Words

Other Redleaf Press books by Carol Garhart Mooney

Swinging Pendulums
Theories of Attachment
Theories of Childhood, Second Edition
Theories of Practice

CHOOSE YOUR WORDS

Communicating with Young Children

SECOND EDITION

Carol Garhart Mooney

Redleaf Press®
www.redleafpress.org
800-423-8309

Published by Redleaf Press
10 Yorkton Court
St. Paul, MN 55117
www.redleafpress.org

© 2005, 2018 by Carol Garhart Mooney

Second edition 2018. The first edition of this work was titled *Use Your Words: How Teacher Talk Helps Children Learn.*
Cover design by Louise OFarrell
Cover photograph by skynesher/iStock
Interior design by Jim Handrigan and Douglas Schmitz
Typeset in Chaparral Pro
Printed in the United States of America
25 24 23 22 21 20 19 18   1 2 3 4 5 6 7 8

Library of Congress Cataloging-in-Publication Data
Names: Mooney, Carol Garhart, author.
Title: Choose your words : communicating with young children / Carol Garhart Mooney.
Other titles: Use your words
Description: Second Edition. | St. Paul, Minnesota : Redleaf Press, [2018] | «The first edition of this work was titled Use Your Words: How Teacher Talk Helps.» | Includes bibliographical references.
Identifiers: LCCN 2017050847 (print) | LCCN 2018001869 (ebook) | ISBN 9781605545271 (ebook) | ISBN 9781605546735 (paperback : acid-free paper)
Subjects: LCSH: Teacher-student relationships. | Interaction analysis in education. | Communication in education. | Oral communication.
Classification: LCC LB1033 (ebook) | LCC LB1033 .M59 2018 (print) | DDC 371.102/3--dc23
LC record available at https://lccn.loc.gov/2017050847

Printed on acid-free paper

This book is dedicated with love and admiration to the memory of Jay Munson (1938–2005), teacher, mentor, and dear friend. It was Jay who taught me to choose my words more carefully!

Contents

Acknowledgments

So many people contribute to the successful publication of a book. My thanks and appreciation go first to the professionals at Redleaf Press. Their knowledge, support, and encouragement are present in every text I have published. This book, however, came to make sense and pull together through the outstanding skill and attitude of my editor, Cathy Broberg. Without her patience, ideas, and encouragement, it would not have gone to press. My inspiration comes from the teachers who routinely share their classrooms and ideas with me, as well as the children in those rooms who tell me their stories. I thank all of the young parents who have shared their ideas about parenting in the twenty-first century.

I am fortunate to have a few friends who year after year support my work. Thank you, Sara, Patrice, Joanne, Karen, Susan, Tessa, Wendy, Cindy, and recently but steadfastly, Mary Ellen and Laura.

Finally, but not at all last, I thank Marc, my husband, best friend, and outstanding administrative assistant. My children, Sean and Johann, Brian, Tom and Angie, and Erin and Gene, have always given love and support and much to think about. My granddaughters, Megan and Caitlin, have given me the opportunity to view development in the twenty-first century—and my grandson, Liam, brings energy, delight, and enthusiasm to my life while forcing me to keep my eyes on change and the future.

Introduction to the Second Edition

MORE THAN A DECADE AGO, I wrote a small book for early educators and child care providers. It was called *Use Your Words: How Teacher Talk Helps Children Learn.* The book was to be a brief reminder to teachers to think about the way they use words with young children. Early on, I made the point that children look to us to be meaning makers. I continue to passionately believe that fact.

In 2018, however, I don't think it is such a simple topic to cover in a small volume. I originally started the first edition after a week when I visited several child care centers and at every single one, adults walked through the space saying, "Use your words, use your words, use your words. . . ." It didn't matter whether a child was crying because he couldn't finish his puzzle, whether she wanted to play and a friend said no, whether someone had just run into her block structure, or whether a parent had slipped out without saying good-bye. The universal response to children shouting, crying, or wailing seemed to be "I can't help you when you do that—use your words." I was impressed by the tiny girl whose answer was "What's my words?" Those of you who were in classrooms ten years ago will remember the trend. Parents and teachers both overused the phrase to a sickening extent. It was a good idea that went awry or was poorly implemented or both.

The kind of challenges I see with children and words and grown-ups might best be introduced through a story. It remains a good way to make a point. I consistently used family and classroom stories in the first edition and will with this edition as well.

At a recent family gathering, my son used the expression "You dropped your sneeze" to his young son who had a bad cold and needed to sneeze but didn't. My grandson immediately leaned over both sides of the tray of his high chair "looking for his sneeze," which is what he would do if he dropped his spoon or his strawberry! My teenaged granddaughters and several others thought this was hysterical. They laughed and laughed. My grandson just looked confused. I'm sure he was. The nature of the confusion will not generate trauma, I'm pretty sure. But continually to be in a state of confusion when adults don't communicate clearly can certainly impede both emotional and social growth. Exposure to a variety of media, changes to the formal use of the English language, and the addition of many new neighbors from around the world make this issue of words and meaning even more important than ever. And it has always been pretty important!

I could not imagine fifteen years ago the daunting task that revising this book seems to me today. We made jokes at Redleaf that we should schedule *Choose Your Words* 3 in a few years, as the newness of all the factors affecting little ones and language are increasing so rapidly that most of us cannot keep up. It is for this reason that *Choose Your Words* offers an additional chapter on contemporary challenges.

Returning to the complexity of children, words, and meaning, after the "dropped sneeze" incident I found myself asking my daughter-in-law more questions about their experience with language and their toddler. I wondered, for example, if they referred to the woodstove as "hot" even if there was no fire lit. After all, how do we adequately, to the best of our ability, make meaning of the world to *all* of the children in our care? Situations are always changing. How do you explain that "hot" changes and that knowing that is really important to a toddler? Why is playing ball in the yard okay but not in the street? How do we explain to small children which contexts allow for shouting and which don't?

Comedians have poked fun at our use of words for decades. My family is full of big fans of comedy and love lines like "Why do they call it a driveway when people park there?" and "Why do they call it a parkway when people drive there?" English is not an easily understood language. It has changed dramatically in the past twenty years for a variety of complex reasons. It is hard to untangle the great variety and yet very different causative factors that make "using words" with children more difficult than it has ever been.

When Urie Bronfenbrenner's *The Ecology of Human Development* was first published in 1979, the work added, in the opinion of many, a critical and unexplored dimension to the study of human psychology. The science had approached many ways of looking at humans, but most of them focused on the individual. Bronfenbrenner changed the way we look at development by stressing the impact of sociology—community, culture, media, government, world events, and point in time. In introducing his ideas, Bronfenbrenner suggested that "public policy has the power to affect the well-being and development of human beings by determining the conditions of their lives" (xiii). Today we realize that we must address context when looking at any piece of research.

I have already used a few examples from the context of my own work and family life to frame some of the challenges that present themselves when we study the use of words with young children. The remaining chapters will do the same, expanding on many of the stories from the first edition as we view them more carefully through a contextual and chronological lens. I will also remind readers of a quote I have used before from my friend and mentor, the late Gwen Morgan, who reminded us that only the complicated can be simplified; the complex requires developing better coping strategies. It was her opinion that we all have spent too much time trying to simplify the complex. The above example of a woodstove is a good one—at least in 2018. When the woodstove is in use, it is hot. When it isn't, it is not. Real logs in the fireplace could be dangerous, though it is now quite common to see restaurants and hotels showing YouTube videos of fires crackling on hearths and fish swimming in fish tanks, neither of which is hot or wet! So if we have an impatient four-year-old who wants to stand near the fire or go see the fish, what do we say?

Neither one is real? They certainly look it! Do we discuss "computer-generated" with a four-year-old? The old expression "things are not always as they seem" seems more relevant today than ever.

We all know that the world has been ever-changing since it began. Since its origin, *Merriam-Webster Dictionary* has been a continual work in progress. Its writers alter, revise, and define or refine language as it develops. It presents for us meaning of the new slang, the newly invented, and the out-of-date. This new edition shares that vision. It raises some questions that have no answers—yet. Chapter 6: Contemporary Challenges has been added to specifically look at some of these questions.

In reworking the pages of *Use Your Words* to present this new edition, *Choose Your Words*, I have attempted to revise or remove that which is no longer relevant, that which time or research has changed, and that which needed more explanation the first time around. I have strived to infuse the chapters with pertinent new learnings. And while respecting those universal pieces that continue to be helpful—so far anyway—I have tried to make sense of the various contexts that encompass language and little ones in the world of 2018.

New Times, New Demands

In the past decade, many of us have struggled with how we meet the demands placed on us by the big changes, sensitive issues, and unanswered challenges that lie before us. We want to be open, but sometimes we feel confused or unprepared. I offer a story from my work life this past year. I was asked to meet with a graduate student of a colleague. She was interested in how the Department of Health and Human Services (DHHS) was making it easier for families new to the United States to transition to urban life in Manchester, New Hampshire. My colleague had given me the name of the student but no other information. I entered the coffee shop at the university looking for Selina. I thought perhaps she was Latina. (Forgive me, but we all bring past experience to our present behaviors.) I stood in the coffee shop, thinking I should have asked for more information when, finally, a lovely woman looking as perplexed as I approached me and said, "Would you be Carol?" Our colleague had not told Selina I was a senior citizen, and she was looking for someone—well, younger! We laughed. We found a table. We admitted what an ironic beginning this was to a meeting regarding the policies and strategies to foster equity in our approach to all families. There are so many large and tiny things for us to consider when we approach differences, and we need to help little ones, in age-appropriate ways, distinguish such differences through language as best we can. Nuances of names and nations are not developmental. They need to be taught and sought by all of us.

Within hours of the national crisis on 9/11 in 2001, the leading friend and advocate of all children, Mr. Fred Rogers, quickly supported adults in helping young children understand what had happened in age-appropriate ways. He was overwhelmed by the reports of young children all over the United States telling parents and teachers that bad people kept running into the skyscrapers in America. "We are getting wrecked," children said. Fred, in comfortable shoes and the right sweater, quietly (as always) and clearly explained that the tragedy had only happened once, but the TV kept showing it over and over again. As previously mentioned, changes in media and technology have altered the way we think, receive, and interpret information. Though children throughout history have experienced trauma and warfare either directly or secondhand from parents or grandparents, 9/11 is perhaps one of the most recent examples of the power of media over children's minds, hearts, fears, and lives.

The issues of media influences and the impact of technology—smartphones and texting—along with continued changes in family life and public education, will be discussed throughout the chapters.

Introduction to the First Edition

This is a book about thinking before we speak! Children count on us to make sense of the world for them. Talking is one of the ways we do this. We do it when we play word games with babies. We point to a nose and say "nose." We point to an ear and say "ear." Books on child development encourage us to provide babies with many examples of meaningful language, to talk to babies about everything they see, and to describe what we are doing for and with them. Most teachers and parents do a pretty good job at this. As children grow past babyhood, however, many of us forget about effectively communicating with them to support their development of language and thinking. Quick, catchy phrases aren't enough to help children make sense of the world. Yet most early childhood teachers and parents use them to excess. We all care about children but fall short of using language that helps them learn the rules of behavior and expectations of culture and classroom that they need to survive in an increasingly complex world. To add to this complexity, a huge percentage of words and ideas children are receiving do not necessarily come from those who care about them, since media is often speaking at children more than their parents or teachers are conversing with them. At a recent conference, I spent a fair amount of time with a Native American man. He said he was fascinated by the way so many of us obsessed over words. "You discuss cursive and manuscript, lined paper or not, word gaps, reading levels, and comprehension levels, yet when my wife and I go out to eat, we often observe families spending the entire time together but not speaking at all. Even toddlers in car seats are using their iPads, children their cell phones. In our community, many stories are oral tradition, funny stories involving gestures used by ancestors for centuries."

When grown-ups don't adequately explain a word, idea, or concept, we put children at a disadvantage. Though respecting children's individuality is a critical part of sensitivity and nurturing all of the children in our care, a goal of exposing children to behavioral expectations and cultural norms of their current community is also part of nurturing their development and success in social and emotional relationships. It is also important to children's sense of continuity (for example, who they are and where they come from) that families put down the iPads and tell funny stories to the children about Aunt Kate who died years before they were born but who remains part of the family history.

USING OUR WORDS AND LANGUAGE LEARNING

We know that children begin to understand language much earlier than they begin to speak. With toddlers we continue to match our use of language to the children's development. We know that children's *receptive language* (the words they understand) is more advanced than their *expressive language* (the words they can say). We know there is a gap between their understanding of a word and their pronunciation of it. The toddler says, "Wawa," and we say, "Yes! Water." We know to set aside the baby talk (sometimes called *motherese* or *parentese*—a high-pitched voice, simple words) that served a sensible social purpose when toddlers were infants.

As children grow, we expect certain developmental milestones, markers like taking first steps, saying first words, or using a cup. We know that children will imitate our use of language, will create some language of their own, and will play with rules of language they are just beginning to understand. We know this from research on language acquisition as well as from listening to children. (For example, see *Language in Early Childhood Education* by Courtney B. Cazden.)

We know that when Jenny says, "I have dogs at my house," her use of the plural demonstrates her knowledge that she has more than one dog. The same is true when her friend Josh says, "The new shoes hurt my footsies." This is also an example of a child *over-regularizing* (using language rules he has learned without regard for subtleties or exceptions) as he experiments in the ongoing process of language learning. Most of us are pretty sensible about supporting language learning in these earliest stages.

But as children develop more and more vocabulary, adults in their lives tend to do less and less modeling and purposeful instruction around language. This is a mistake preschool teachers often make. They assume that the need for *deliberate extension* of language (when parents or teachers expand the children's short sentences such as "Mommy here" to *Mommy is here* or "Baby cry" to *The baby is crying*) is not as necessary now that the children are older and know so many words.

Lilian Katz has said, "Teachers throughout the early years tend to overestimate children academically but underestimate them intellectually" (Katz and Chard 1989, 5). Teachers have similar tendencies with language and preschoolers. We forget that children understand words that they don't yet use and use words that they don't yet fully understand. I am reminded of the child who, when asked how old he was, said, "Can't tell. Got my mittens on!" This was a child who could count to ten or more and could hold up three fingers but didn't yet make the connections among age, numbers, himself, and verbal representation of the three fingers he held up when asked his age. Another example is the exuberant two-year-old I observed in a restaurant who, when asked how old he was by a waiter, gave an engaging smile, proudly held up all five fingers, and said, "I'm two!" Again, this little one was making connections to himself, his age, words, and counting—but not all pieces were neatly tied together yet. Quite sadly, I have seen well-meaning adults (both parents and teachers) change happy moments like this into an "out of context" teachable moment. Rather than verifying the joy the child was feeling that he sure knew how old he was, many of us say, "Now this is two—can you put these three fingers down like Auntie?" This response is helpful to an older preschooler but doesn't help a toddler understand concepts of mathematics or how old she is. Jeannette Stone's (2002) story below further illustrates this point.

In the 1960s, Stone was teaching in a Head Start program. She told me this story: "I realized as I said, 'I'll need you to take turns,' that the children had no idea what taking turns meant. So I had to teach them. First Sherry will use the swing. When she's done, Jack can use the swing. This is what we call taking turns.'" Stone's insight is something many of us lack when talking with young children. We often assume children understand when they don't. We sometimes say things like "Be polite," "Use your manners," "Behave," "Be sweet," or "That's rude," concepts that many adults could not adequately describe to another adult, much less a child. The first time we take up residence with anyone who was not raised where and how we were, the experience is quite startling. We quickly become aware that what was considered polite to us is considered aloofness by others. What was thought of as sensible to us is thought of as crazy by others. Whether it is barracks, a dormitory, shared apartment renters, or a new spouse or partner, it takes time to figure out the new social norms and to respect each other's differing approach to life.

For children, that's what every day is like. I remember taking my oldest two children to Jordan Marsh for a fancy holiday lunch. They were all dressed up and excited, actually doing a great job of acting like they dined out on a frequent basis. My oldest made what he thought was wonderful conversation with the woman at the table next to us. In his most polite, grown-up voice, he said to this lovely sixty-ish and somewhat obese woman, "You know, my mother used to be bigger—not like you—but bigger. She went to Weight Watchers and it really helped." The woman gathered her things and left immediately. I was mortified but stared straight ahead.

A colleague shared a story of a relative's cross-country flight with a very young child—not an easy job! She took occasional breaks walking up and down the aisle with her little one. Suddenly the child stopped short, staring at a bald man in an aisle seat. With the booming voice of a small child who has just made a huge and unusual discovery, he shouted, "You have no hair on your head!"

Then there was the time I took a class of kindergartners to Boston to view the world from the top of the newly built Prudential Center. We were a group of nearly twenty, including several volunteer parents. The elevator's capacity is about forty. The next person in was a middle-aged man in a wheelchair. One of our children shouted, "Holy mackerel—you got no legs! Where did they go?" All of our volunteers gasped loudly and looked at my coteacher and me—expecting I'm not sure what! The man smiled a huge and charming smile. He looked right in the eyes of the little boy, ignoring the rest of us, and said, "Thanks, son, for asking. So many people look away and try to act like

I'm not here at all. I had an accident in a job I was doing a long time ago. I'm fine. It doesn't hurt. You should see what I can do with this chair. I'll show you when we get up there!"

Each of the above examples is a typical story of the way young children use their words. As adults, we have been conditioned not to be so open, emotionally honest, and direct as children are when they are just getting used to the world around them. For us the challenge remains what needs to be let go, what needs to be responded to, and, if so, how? It all depends on the situation, the age and developmental level of the child, and so on. The words we choose to use in providing understanding that supports children is based on all of these things but also must always be individualized.

Solutions and strategies to these interesting dilemmas will be explored throughout the text.

WHAT TO EXPECT FROM THIS TEXT

Chapter 1 looks specifically at "teacher talk" and how it supports or complicates children's learning and the world around them.

Chapter 2 looks at giving directions and instructions and assessing whether we have been successful in our attempts to accomplish these tasks with the young children in our lives.

Chapter 3 looks at correcting behavior. The meaning of behavior in the context of the lives of very young children is basically "What they are doing right now." What words can we choose to help them connect their words and actions with our, sometimes truly necessary, directives?

Chapter 4 looks at appropriate curriculum in language learning for very young children and addresses some of the ways teacher talk and planning affects the response of early educators to "push down" curriculum and its effects on children and families.

Chapter 5 stresses the importance of plain old talking. Many of our young children have few opportunities to develop this very essential skill. The chapter focuses on conversations, discussions, and storytelling. It also briefly discusses the morphing of language into a whole new action as a result of rapid technological change and continual device use by most Americans.

Chapter 6 offers thoughts on the context within which the tasks of the other five chapters must be accomplished. It discusses the contemporary challenges that make all of these tasks pose such difficult questions *and* such exciting opportunities.

Many pieces of basic language teaching and learning seem as old as time. When teachers are not clear, children don't learn, or, worse, they experience confusion or embarrassment because they don't know what to do. Sometimes when children don't know what to do, they engage in behaviors that adults find inconvenient or difficult. Yet often adults do not make the connection between the way we speak and the way children act. The purpose of this book is to help make that connection. The way we use and choose our words can truly help children know what is expected, understand their world, and manage within it quite a bit better. This sounds exactly like what my teachers tried to do for us in the 1950s. But this is increasingly important because of the number and diversity of many very young children who are new to the United States. Often white, middle-class teachers think of culture as Irish or French, Mexican or Syrian but don't think about the "family culture" each of us brings to whatever we do (Delpit 1995). We are all different from each other in many ways, and we are all the same in many ways. A good rule of thumb if we are trying to be meaning makers for young children is to assume nothing. Start at the beginning. Keep it simple. Repeat important messages frequently. My first model, Sister Mary Catherine, said repeatedly, "Repetition is the mother of all learning!" So much has changed, but for young children, I think that the need for frequent repetition has not.

The way teachers use their words can also make their own days less frustrating. Children want to cooperate with us. They want to know what we expect from them. When we take the time to think before we speak—to choose our words with care—our chances for clarity improve. When we are clear, children are more cooperative.

This makes life easier for all of us and is worth the time and reflection involved.

The ideas presented here are not new. As you read this book, I'm sure you will find yourself saying, "I know that." A trip through most preschools, however, shows us that we all still need to remind ourselves to choose our words more carefully and to embrace thoughtful change with enthusiasm.

CHAPTER ONE

Teacher Talk
and Children's Learning

A COLLEAGUE RECENTLY SHARED WITH ME one of those "children and language" stories that parents and teachers love to collect. The director was giving a prospective family a tour of her building. In the middle of the tour, her assistant interrupted, saying there was an important phone call. The director apologized, saying she had to take the call. Getting down to the child's level, she smiled and said, "This is Nancy. She'll show you our preschool room in the meantime." The child looked alarmed and said politely, "No, thank you. I want to go to the nice time, not the mean time!"

These are the stories we all find so charming. *Reader's Digest* used to offer parents fifty or seventy-five dollars for allowing the inclusion of such stories in the monthly family pages. But these stories are far more than cute. They are indicators to us of how easily very young children are confused by our casual use of language. This is also a reason to remember that sarcasm is lost on young children. We offer more confusion if, in our frustration, we make comments like, "Well, I hope you're happy now." Children need for us to continue to provide meaning and definitions for the thousands of words we use every day. We need to repeat those definitions and extend the meaning as children grow. It's helpful to avoid expressions like (1) "It's raining cats and dogs," (2) "She was born with a silver spoon in her mouth" (usually not spoken to but within hearing distance of children), (3) "They bent over backwards for her," (4) "The noise was so scary it made my hair stand on end," or (5) "He sure has ants in his pants."

Children need for us to continue to provide meaning and definitions for the thousands of words we use every day. We need to repeat those definitions and extend the meaning as children grow.

We need to offer, instead, a direct, fairly simple explanation for ordinary words, objects, and actions. We need to regularly remind new and veteran teachers, as well as ourselves, that the tiniest infant needs conversation, smiles, and animation from us. When we watch carefully, we see how much we can learn from each individual baby. We are having conversations. Throughout the book, the discussion is repeated that facial expressions, eye contact, body language, and general attitude are interpreted and felt by the youngest of children. This is where language development begins. Below is a story that clearly demonstrates this point:

Michelle is an Early Head Start teacher who understands the need for all this defining and repetition. All day she talks to and with the children. She asks interesting questions, though her mostly nonverbal children don't answer—*yet!* Each routine, story, and activity is accompanied by many, many words. I listened with delight one day to Michelle's conversation while she was changing a diaper. Timmy was almost two, learning new things every day. Michelle knew that diapering was not one of his favorite things. "I will try to make this quick, Timmy," she said respectfully. "I know you don't like having to leave your play."

As she changed him, she talked about the process and then elaborated, "Now all I have to do is pull up your pants. Your pants keep your legs warm. I wore my pants today to keep my legs warm. We are wearing pants." The diapering was done. Timmy got down, walked back into the room, looked at me very seriously, and said, "Pants!" This might seem a simple thing, yet I am amazed at the missed opportunities many teachers let pass right by when they could be defining the ordinary but very necessary information about mundane things in our daily lives to which we nonetheless need to put words. Those of us who work with infants and toddlers need to make this a continual approach to teaching the very young.

To expand this story, I'd also like to call attention to a few things quite relevant to our discussion. Michelle is a master teacher. She received her associate of arts degree in early childhood education from a college respected for its teacher training. She came to her job with experience as a mother and as a family child care provider. When she joined the Head Start faculty, she was totally committed to her choice of career.

It is not an accident that she said respectfully, "I'll try to make this fast, Timmy" *before* she said, "I know you don't like to leave your play." She did not want to provide a reason for a negative reaction before he thought it up himself. She was matter of fact. She did not apologize for interrupting as, after all, she was giving him quality care by keeping him dry and comfortable. She did not ask his permission but was caring and respectful as she proceeded with doing what needed to be done: giving him a clean diaper. Then she made the very best of the situation by explaining what was going on and expanding the meaning of the word *pants*. This may not seem extremely profound, but you'd be amazed at the number of heartbreaking meltdowns I have observed when, without thinking, teachers say, "Do you mind if I change your pants now?" All toddler teachers know the favorite word of those working very hard at developing their independence: "NO!" Or, more accurately, "NO NO NO NO!" Again and again we must remind ourselves not to give a choice when there isn't one!

What Is at Stake?

In the example about the "mean time," not much damage was done. But as I write these words in February of one of New England's worst winters in years, I think of three-and-a-half-year-old Sita clutching her snowsuit. When I entered the room yesterday, she was sitting in her cubby, sobbing and kicking. The two teachers were upset and puzzled by this unexpected behavior. As I observed, the volunteer grandmother took over trying to calm Sita, and the two teachers continued their debate about taking children outside.

The first teacher said, "So many kids are getting sick. They need fresh air."

Her colleague responded, "But with snow this deep, how can we watch them? They'll disappear!"

It didn't take long for me to connect Sita's sobbing (she usually loved outdoor play) with the murky notion that she could disappear and never be found!

This is something demanding more thought from all of us. Every early childhood textbook cautions beginning teachers against talking about the children as if they are not listening and watching adults' every move. Yet it's easy to do this without giving any thought to our words or their consequences. All of these phrases have been spoken over children's heads in my workplace in the past month:

- "Do you think she needs the nebulizer?"

- "She feels hot. Should we call the nurse?"

- "He seems so tired. I hope we don't have a hard time settling him for nap."

- "Did he have mittens when he arrived? I can't find any in his cubby."

- "Watch her—she's been biting Heather every chance she gets!"

I work with programs accredited by the National Association for the Education of Young Children (NAEYC) in which well-educated teachers care deeply about children and teaching. None of the above statements are particularly unprofessional, yet each violates the basic premise that we should not talk about children in their presence as if they are not there. Imagine yourself in the position of a small child listening to powerful adults discuss you this way over your head. Would you feel afraid if you heard them discussing your difficulty breathing? If you heard that you might have a hard time settling down to sleep, how would that affect you when you lay down on your mat? Would hearing that you've been biting every chance you get make you feel more or less in control, more or less frustration? How do these phrases make it easier or harder for teachers and children to manage the common classroom challenges they represent?

Adults have a much more sophisticated understanding of the world than children do. They have the capacity for abstract thinking, while children's thinking is literal. Though human developmentalists would assert that adults have capacity for abstract thinking and young children do not, many scholars today fear that it's much more complicated than that. It is refreshing that serious researchers today frequently acknowledge the complexity of the issues we face with children, families, education, and the sociological context that have not been such a big piece of the picture until recently. When children who are so young that they are not yet fluent in the language of their families are thrust into a school situation where they must try to manage a second language in addition to their first, culture, competence, and common sense clash. When children are hungry, cold, exhausted, or traumatized, language learning is not as easy as ABC. We have much to contemplate. The situation demands supports that few programs are fortunate to have enough of. We know the needs are critical for experienced and competent language teachers, for family service workers, and for native language interpreters who understand not only the language but the needs, development, and typical behaviors of the children they are working with. It is a tall order. We are working on it and see great progress compared to a decade ago, but we still have a long, long way to go.

The above factors are as critical to finding solutions to our current challenges as the wisdom provided by Edward Zigler, Joseph Stone, Urie Bronfenbrenner, and others when they finally convinced Congress in establishing Head Start that it wasn't as easy as ABCs!

Adults whose first language is English have internalized many English idioms and shortcuts that are very confusing to young children. For children or adults whose home language is not English, the challenges are even more complicated and frustrating. The fact is that we don't have a long list of viable strategies for making this professional challenge disappear anytime in the near future. And most of us don't want to admit or discuss how scared it makes us feel. The efforts of so many who have invested time, energy, and nurturing sensitivity to provide training on cultural competence and sensitivity have helped all of us pay attention to how serious our challenges are. They have provided us with day-to-day examples of how our well-intentioned efforts don't necessarily help in the way we intend or hope. Our missed steps with language and children go way beyond cultural sensitivity or a strong understanding of child growth and development. They actually contribute to uncertainty that we could eliminate if we reflected on these issues more frequently. Here are some more examples of language frequently used but rarely helpful to the complex and complicated task before us:

- Was she raised in a barn?

- I'm not telling her. I got burned last month for that.

- We've got problems now—the computer crashed!

- Right! That will happen when pigs fly!

- I think she got up on the wrong side of the bed.

- Lots of problems in that house!

- Who says something like that?

In other words, each of us grows up in some family context. This could be a foster family; communal family; single- or dual-parent family; gay or lesbian family; upper-income, middle-income, or economically struggling family. The neighborhood, geographic location, and extended family situations all add another layer of complexity to where and how we moved from birth to age eighteen or thirty. Culture and ethnicity are part of it, but basic human differences are probably a bigger part. It is human nature for most of us to, initially, believe that what we experienced is *reality*. But the true reality is that there are many, many realities. There are overlapping realities. There are oppositional realities. There are values and traditions that are the essence of some families and are unknown to others. None of us owns the one true reality of how things are. None of us owns what it means to be a family. Yet most of us in this country grew up thinking, at least for a while, that our way was *the* way. It is a joyful reality that the twenty-first century has brought technological, diverse cultural and political realities to the table that force all of us to think beyond ourselves and our community or country to interpret more of our learnings in a global way than we did in decades past. We are all right—sometimes. We are all wrong sometimes. What is right and wrong is debatable a fair amount of the time. Difference is reality. We all need to learn to embrace that. So what we teach children is essential.

It isn't always easy, but it is essential to our ability to teach the next generation to accept differences. One might ask what this has to do with language learning and children. It is a fair question. The possibilities of answers will be uncomfortable or even unacceptable to many of us reared in an ethnocentric environment where we were conditioned to believe that our way was *the* way. It challenges us to accept that change is necessary. If we want children to learn a language of acceptance of differences, a language of inclusion, then we need to learn to accept that ourselves. For some of us, that might be a challenge we do not choose to take on personally; nonetheless, we must do so professionally.

For very young children, this is not the challenge it is for us. They are not yet conditioned to believe one thing over another. They have to be carefully taught. This places on our shoulders a great responsibility to children everywhere and to live more mindfully. I can offer a fun alternative to the study of cultural differences or futuristic plans for world peace. See if you can find the 1958 edition of *South Pacific*, and watch and listen carefully to the song "Carefully Taught."

Think for a moment about the images the above-cited common statements from teachers conjure up for a three- or four-year-old who takes every statement at face value. To a preschooler, the word *crash* describes something you do on bikes or in a car accident. It is a forceful physical event accompanied by noise, broken glass, and crumpled metal, or your friend crying because you ran your bike over her toe. What meaning can this young child make of a computer crash?

If we go back to Sita screaming in her cubby, we can generate many questions for a concerned teacher to ask:

- Is she feeling threatened because we don't seem to know what to do and are arguing about it in front of her?
- What is her understanding of *disappear*?

- Am I mistaking fear for misbehavior or lack of cooperation?

- What has she seen or heard on TV or radio about the disappearance of a child or parent?

- Have I tried to console her or said, "You're okay, Sita," without asking why she's upset?

> Adults have a much more sophisticated understanding of the world than children do. They have the capacity for abstract thinking, while preschoolers' thinking is still very literal.

Sita's teachers were focused on two things: making the decision about outdoor play and trying to get a squirming, screaming little one into a snowsuit. Although both are part of a day's work with young children, these teachers were missing their point for being involved in this work—to help children understand the world around them.

What could they have done instead? The conversation about when or whether to go outside because of the temperature and depth of snow might have taken place early in the morning before the children arrived. This is part of the daily planning process. Before children arrive, teachers can speak together in a brief or abbreviated way that they understand but young children might not. This avoids confusion for children.

If that didn't happen, the teachers might have thought about Sita's unusual reaction and tried to figure out what it meant. Since they knew her well, they knew she loved her time in the outdoors.

If she's not too upset to talk, the first thing to do would be to ask Sita, "What is this about?" That might have ended the situation. I remember walking in on little Evan in tears early in the morning and saying, "Are you missing Mom this morning?" Quickly he rubbed his eyes and said, "Nope. Cook let me help do onions for our soup, and they gotted in my eyes!" So often adults make wrong assumptions about what children are thinking and feeling. If teachers take the time to investigate the meaning of children's behavior by asking them about it, children are often able to tell them what's going on.

If teachers say something foolish or simply thoughtless, it is easy enough to backtrack. In this situation, the teachers could have said something like, "I was being silly, Sita. We won't disappear. It's just that the snow is very, very deep. Chris and I were just talking about being able to watch all of you as you play in that deep, deep snow. Can I help you with your snowsuit? I know how you love to play in the snow."

An additional example offers the power of modeling, both for children and novice teachers:

I observed an excellent instance of this kind of language clarification recently in an Early Head Start classroom in which all of the children are just beginning to use language and understand consequences. An assistant teacher made the classic mistake of saying to a young two-year-old, "Would you like to join us for lunch now, Kahlil?" Her lead teacher, modeling well for both the child and the assistant teacher, scooped him up and said tactfully, "We confused you, Kahlil. That sounded like a choice, but it's time to eat. I'll help you find your seat." He smiled, settled in, and sipped his soup.

This example shows how easily teacher talk can confuse children, the kind of regrouping we can do when we know it has happened, and the child's cooperative response to clear directions and knowing what is expected of him. This, of course, like much we wish we could do better, cannot always be changed. For many of us, a good beginning might be journaling or really thinking about the words we choose and how we use them with the children in our lives. Most of us say many things out of habit or because we heard things done this way over and over in our own lives or school years. Often, we are completely unaware—until a precocious three-year-old looks at us with curiosity and says, "What are you talking about?"

When we talk with young children, we use language for a variety of reasons. Our hope is to increase the child's vocabulary, model the correct pronunciation, make meaning, and provide contexts for the thousands of words we use every day. Several specific functions of language that teachers frequently have in mind when communicating with children are addressed throughout these pages. These are

- to provide direction or give instructions,
- to correct and redirect behavior,
- to develop concepts and skills,

- to discuss classroom or family life, and

- to assist all children in learning skills to prepare them for the lifelong pursuit of meaning in language—their own and those of others in their lives.

Throughout the day, teachers need to inform children about what's coming next or tell them what's expected of them. When teachers are not precise, their vague directions confuse children and can lead to misunderstandings. This is especially the case for children new to this country or new to this center. We try to give adults orientation when they are new to our program. Yet often three- or four-year-olds are popped into a group of peers with no explanation of routines, expectations, choices, and the like. I have spent many years in the past four decades observing students and practicing teachers. Our profession seems to attract clichés like honey attracts bees! Here are a few examples:

- 1-2-3. . . all eyes on me

- crisscross applesauce

- listening ears

- indoor voices

- cleanup time. Sing your song!

Imagine, if you can, a child who joins your program in February and observes the entire building moving—as we think of mass robot movement—when a grown-up says "crisscross applesauce," but she has no idea what these little cues mean. My favorite is when the lights go out and everyone freezes! A new school is a big enough challenge. Adding a language not even related to her home language or to the new language she is trying to understand since she moved here is simply too much to ask.

I remember my first day as a director in a small school. I have always loved music and usually play a variety of it in the background during the day. Children were happily busy at their play. I put on the music, and immediately the children stopped what they were doing and hurried to the group area where they sat "crisscross applesauce" and looked at me expectantly. I wasn't sure what had just happened, so I smiled and said, "What now?" One of the older children said, "You put music on." "Yes, I did," I responded. "I thought you might enjoy it!" I do enjoy many of the ways children speak up today in a way my generation never would have. This same boy said, quite kindly and patiently, "You are new here. You could use some help. We do many things here. We have choices. When you put on music, we know it is time to change what we are doing. So we come here. But you don't say, 'What now?' We do. Then you tell us!" This exchange is an example of one of the finer pieces of staff orientation I have ever experienced.

> Our hope is to increase the child's vocabulary, model the correct pronunciation, and make meaning that provides context for the thousands of words we use every day.

Redirecting behavior is one of the most important functions of language in the early years and also one of the most frequently misused! We do not mean to give the wrong messages to young children, but we frequently do. I fear some of the confusion began when teacher training started focusing on creating more authoritative (democratic) classrooms to replace a tendency toward authoritarian approaches in previous decades. I have had student teachers tell me their training has encouraged them to take their cues from children and not to tell them what to do. I would agree that this is a fine approach in many contexts—but not all contexts. Picture a toddler, new to your program, having a grown-up pop a painting smock over her head (they do look a bit like a bib—and have the same purpose!), walk her over to a tiny easel with a tray of cups full of brightly colored "stuff," and say enthusiastically, "Now you can paint!" There is not a toddler who will respond, "I'm sorry, Teacher . . . what is paint? Do I eat or drink this? Why aren't I at the table? I'm really confused. Just what do you want me to do with all of this great-looking stuff?" I have had many parents tell me over the years that they love what the children do at school because then they don't have to deal with the mess of playdough, fingerpaint, ooblick, and so on. We cannot assume children have any idea what the materials we are using are. They need to be carefully taught. "This is paint. This is a brush. I put this extra shirt on you so you can keep much of the paint on the paper instead of your shirt. Sometimes we call it a smock."

As teachers of young children, we are usually very excited about sharing concepts and assisting children in developing necessary skills. Too often, however, we think of skill development in too narrow a way. Many teachers assume that concept development means such things as short and tall, colors, shapes, letters, numbers, sink and float. More critical to school and life readiness are practical skills such as Jeannette Stone's (2002) example of taking turns. We must teach the typical academic skills of the preschool years. Both parents and administrators expect this from us, as they should. But the social and practical skills children need to understand and function in the world around them are equally critical to their future life's success.

Children need our help learning to use tools, words, their bodies. We need to take the necessary time to discuss and help each other learn strategies that will support children's development of knowledge. It is also critical that we all acknowledge that teachers are up against dramatic pushes from respected national publications, administrators who are often under pressure from superintendents, and research that reaches practitioners, on average, twenty years after it has raised an issue and conscientious practitioners begin taking the information seriously (Hart and Risley 1995). We are in an area where everything moves so quickly that we make choices without timely consideration of the consequences for children and families. We quickly adapt decisions whose research may not really meet the needs of the families we serve. It is often not comfortable for teachers to have to regroup the way they do things with no opportunity to reflect, plan, or get used to this new implementation of ideas or curriculum—or even lunch schedules!

A good way to prevent this "forging ahead" mentality is to slow down. Many teachers and administrators believe that they are not really working for their wages if they spend time in mindful conversation with colleagues and self-reflection. These are two of the most significant strategies to change the direction of our "push down, hurry up, keep going" approach that helps us feel defeated and certainly does not help the children and families who are the heartfelt focus of our work.

Discussing classroom and family events provides teachers with many opportunities to expand both language and understanding for children. The United States is an increasingly diverse country. Teachers are serving children from many countries, family situations, and economic backgrounds. Americans are tremendously diverse in the ways they live at home and the things they think are important. It is not uncommon for *ethnocentrism* (thinking the way one culture or class or family does things is the only or the best way) to affect teachers' conversations and approaches with children and families. This calls for us to think before we speak.

The discussion on classroom events and family life will include tips to help teachers develop a repertoire of skills for navigating turbulent waters involving differing family values and ideas. This is a very complex task. It is not one for which there is a single answer. The answers, like the questions, are many. No one knows everything. Everyone is capable of making a gigantic misstep. Our job is to realize it, apologize if relevant or helpful, and keep up our daily struggle to support families who depend on us. I don't remember who said it, but I am fond of the expression that the only true mistake is one we don't learn from. We need to have the courage to make a statement, to try to help— even if, upon reflection, it wasn't the best idea in the world! Families appreciate and need our sincere efforts to help them navigate these tough parental waters.

Basic Guidelines

Where do we start? This text offers some time-tested and also some differing strategies to use when talking with children. It is not intended to tell you how you should be whenever you are guiding young children. It is gatherings from many teachers, texts, classrooms, and children who have shared with me. I thank them for sharing and have pulled ideas together to share with you. Here are some basic guidelines that will help you begin to think more clearly about your conversations with children in the classroom. Your conversations will be part of language acquisition for the children you teach. The suggestions below come from many places and many teachers. You will know which ones fit your style and the families you work with.

- Make sure you have the child's attention before you begin to speak. A gentle hand on her arm might help, depending on the child and the situation. Children are so different. Some do not like to be touched. Others are listening intently without establishing eye contact. Slowing down is a fabulous strategy for using language and also for joining new groups or getting to know people (children, their families, our coworkers). It is a strategy that is good for thinking, making decisions, breathing, rearranging areas of the classroom, and resolving conflicts! Many of us remember when we could not be reached by phone if we were driving, and we recall when the only way we could make tea was when the water boiled on the stove! Today we can put a K-Cup in a Keurig and in seconds be sipping our favorite tea. We can email or text family and friends in other states and resolve travel plans at once. Physicians can send lab work from Boston to Los Angeles in minutes. All of this makes living easier. But we can't transfer this efficient immediacy to human growth or relationships. Trust takes time. Friendship takes time. Most babies crawl before they walk and babble before they talk. Those of us who work with growing children need to repeat the message, to all who will listen, that childhood is a journey, not a race. It is refreshing to see the number of young sociologists, psychologists, physicians, philosophers, and physical education professionals who are all joining with one voice to say "Slow down!"

- Always get down to a child's level when talking to her. If sitting on the floor or squatting is uncomfortable for you, try keeping a chair handy. If you were two feet tall, someone six feet three or even five feet three would look like a giant. We all agree on the extent to which tone of voice, facial expression, and eye contact enhance or detract from verbal communication. These are tiny things we can do to greatly enhance the power and effectiveness of our conversations with young children.

- Use simple words and short sentences. Avoid idioms and short-cuts. Try to say exactly what you mean as clearly as possible.

- Don't be wishy-washy. If you mean no, say it. If you say no, mean it! This is the most critical time for you to align tone of voice, facial expression, and body language with the words you're using.

- Don't ask a question or offer a choice when there isn't one. Let children know clearly what you need from them. In particular, avoid using "okay?" at the end of directives, as in "It's cleanup time, okay?" or "Please put that down, okay?" To say, "Do you know what I mean?" is very different. It offers the child an opportunity to shake her head one way or another or say yes or no. It clarifies your expectation. When we say "okay?" we are changing an expectation to a choice.

- Don't ask questions to which you already know the answer. This applies to managing behavior as well as concept development. Don't ask a child, "Is that the way we treat our friends?" You already know that pushing another child is not a good way to treat him, but a young child may not yet. Likewise, there are better ways to develop children's thinking skills than to ask them questions about numbers and colors and letters to which you already know the answer.

- If you must interrupt children, remember they deserve the same courtesy adults expect. Say something like, "Excuse me, I need you in the book corner now, please." Teach *please, thank you, I'm sorry, you're welcome*, and other niceties by your own modeling rather than prodding with that old "What do you say?"

- Use praise in moderation and only when it is sincere and truly called for. When you are praising a child, be specific. For example, instead of just saying, "Good job!" follow it with the appreciated behavior: "Good job picking up the blocks." Better yet, avoid praise altogether, and comment on or thank the child for the work she did. For example, "You did a lot of work picking up those blocks," or "Thank you for picking up so many blocks. Look how much space there is now!"

Discussion Questions

1. Can you think of a time when a child was trying to tell you something important but you missed it because you focused on the wrong thing? What clues did the child give you that might have helped? What questions might you have asked to get at the child's concerns?

2. Why do you think teachers often avoid having difficult or controversial conversations with children? What difficult topics have come up when you are working with children? How might you handle them in the future?

3. When do you tend to ask children questions that you already know the answer to? What is your purpose when you find yourself doing this—to manage behavior? To instruct? To find out what a child knows? How could you accomplish your purpose in a different way? What can you do to remind yourself to do it less frequently?

4. Has your district or center held trainings to support staff in becoming more culturally sensitive? Discuss the interesting points of agreement and disagreement. Have you reflected on the fact that every family has its own culture? Think of assumptions we make about others when we don't really have any idea if they are true. Could you devote an entire staff meeting to discussing this in relation to your entire group of children?

5. Does your program offer current training in technological changes that parents might be worried about and seeking answers to? If not, do you have a suggestion box? How can you work as a team to foster ongoing learning that helps meet family needs?

CHAPTER TWO

Giving Direction and Instructions

THROUGHOUT THE DAY in early childhood classrooms, teachers need to give children direction and instructions. How and when this is accomplished greatly affects the growth of both children's understanding and language skills. When teachers are vague, use catchphrases, or imply information rather than stating it explicitly, children are apt to be confused. Confused children may be anxious or rebellious. They may comply to the best of their ability silently or resist instruction. In either case, they are not learning what they could be, and their feelings may well get in the way of their ability to take in more information. These patterns create a negative cycle that can affect children into their elementary school years and beyond. The following are examples of this cycle:

- If a child is confused, she may push at another child because she's frustrated.

- Another will find something to do that is *not* confusing—like opening and closing the Velcro on his shoes, thus tuning out on classroom goings-on.

- Others might just decide, ever so early, that preschool or learning stinks.

One area in which many of us communicate in ways that seem vaguer than usual is when we provide children access to creative activities. This probably goes back to some of the old "let children blossom" philosophy, which avoided teacher directions for almost anything. When presenting creative art activities to children, we have all been taught not to draw pictures for children and not to present teacher-made models for the product of the art activity. This is often appropriate, but unfortunately many times the use of materials needs to be clearly explained to children or the consequences can be dire. Also, we should remember that twenty paper-plate bunnies with the cottontail glued in exactly the same place is not too creative. A trip to a local gallery, a walk in the woods, and an invitation to do a still life of ferns and forsythia might be!

I am reminded of an art activity involving spatter painting. The teacher involved was excited about this activity, which involved taping a cutout of an autumn leaf onto a piece of easel paper and letting the children spatter red, yellow, and orange paint around it to create a background. She demonstrated for the children how to hold the brush and flick it a little, sending a spatter of paint across the paper. This was a good start. She both instructed the children and showed them what to do. In this case, however, knowing how children love process and experimentation, the teacher should have said a few words about what *not* to do. Thinking she had her bases covered, she left the children at the easel and moved on to other areas. The loud giggling and shouts soon drew her back to the easels to find that children were spattering the walls, the floor, and each other. This inexperienced teacher then understandably thought the children were misbehaving, when in reality they were simply deeply engaged in the activity she had provided for them without giving enough clear instruction about the process!

The answer is not to avoid giving direction or instruction—that would be impossible. The answer is twofold: you can pay attention to being clear, direct, and precise in your instructions and directions to children, and you can assume that children who did not follow directions did not understand them and go from there.

Here is a story of a very similar activity that could have gone awry but did not because the teacher recognized the possibility for too much experimentation and carefully explained the activity to the children. Lori had seen an activity she thought the children would find interesting. It was a kind of texture painting created by filling a piece of panty hose with popcorn kernels, tying a knot, and then dabbing, rolling, or dotting the paint onto the paper. I was fascinated but also impressed as Lori took time to explain to the children that the hose pieces were not to be swung in the air, used anyplace except on the paper, untied, or used in any way other than as a paint applicator. "Does everyone know what I need you to do?" she asked.

It's such a simple sentence—"Does everyone know what I need you to do?"—yet it can clarify so much. The activity went quite well. Lori observed, however, that the materials were almost as interesting to the children as the painting activity. The children, understandably, had probably never played with panty hose before and found the texture, stretchability, and feel of popcorn inside to be quite engaging. Observing carefully, she was able to keep the children on task with the painting while acknowledging their fascination with this particular paint applicator. "I'll fill some more while you finish painting," she said. "Then when we go outside, we'll see what else you can do with them. There is more space outside, and we won't use paint!" The children were delighted. Outside they stretched, pulled, played catch, and had contests throwing them up in the air and across the field.

This story illustrates a teacher listening to the children and following their lead, yet preventing mess, harm, or out-of-control responses to what truly was an interesting, creative activity. Considering all of that potential for experimentation and learning, she took the materials to another place and allowed children to use them in another way that the children also loved. Lori understood that the four-year-olds were bound to swing the materials around inside, spattering the walls and each other, if she handed them to the children without adequate discussion of how to use them. She understood that it was her job, not the children's, to set the boundaries for the use of the materials.

Sadly, I have worked with many teachers who think children's spirits are stolen by boundaries. Not so. Remember: we are meaning makers. What would happen if we had no stoplights in busy cities? What would happen if children were taught the world would stop in order to keep them safe? It won't. We need rules. We need boundaries—and we need to know who's in charge. For the young children in our care, the answer to that last one is *us*!

Being clear and firm when necessary without being overbearing or stifling is a delicate balance. Sharing in our daily example and using words, materials, and wonderful children's literature are positive, often nonverbal ways of teaching about boundaries. In the resource section, you will find many of these resources.

Giving Specific Direction

One of the important goals during preschool is to help children begin to process directions. Clarity is important when teaching children to follow directions, so many teachers offer first a simple, one-step direction and then advance in complexity as a child's understanding increases. Still, there are times when we assume the child is not complying when the actual problem is in the way we phrase the direction. Remember the point already discussed but worth repeating: if we add the word *okay* to the end of an instruction, it turns a directive into a choice.

Think about the times during the day when you need to give children directions. You may need them to sit quietly for a circle time or a story; you may need them to line up to go to the bathroom or outside. I have known teachers who believe there is *never a reason* to ask children to line up. There is a genuine need in our field to give each other a bit more understanding and flexibility. If you are in a well-funded program where two of you support ten children and have toilets in your room, your demands and directions can be very different from a first-grade teacher in a building that houses pre-K to grade six students where toilets are down the hall. Days without an assistant require different routines. You may need the children to approach new materials in a certain way. Whatever the situation, the more specific your directions, the more successful you and the children are likely to be. Unfortunately, many of the common directives teachers give children—the things we say without even thinking about it—are not specific enough for children to understand. In addition, many teachers rely on abstract concepts and social norms that children have not yet had the experience to develop.

For example, have you ever heard a teacher ask children to "sit nicely"? These words are vague and mean different things to different children and families. In addition, *nice* is an abstract concept. Young children are literal thinkers, and they need lots of time, many experiences, and probably some direct instruction to internalize what an abstract word like *nice*, *good*, *cooperative*, *friendly*, or *kind* means. It is also true that we all grow, taking on ideas or characteristics such as kind, sensible, funny, mean, important, and so on. from the adults in our lives, families, schools, communities, or cultures. There is no one right way.

Teachers are sometimes concerned to hear, "There is no right way." Obviously, there is a right way to drink out of a cup without spilling. It takes time to learn, yet spilling is still a risk whenever drinking out of a cup. Being open to new ways, mistakes, more mistakes, and different ideas is critical for enthusiastic lifelong learners. When giving young children directions, be brief and specific: "Sit on your bottom, and don't touch anyone else. Please be quiet so everyone can hear the story and see the pictures."

Here are some of the phrases teachers often use with children. I'm sure you've heard several of them in the last twenty-four hours!

- Be kind.
- Be cooperative.
- Be polite.
- Quiet down.
- Walking feet.
- Listening ears.
- Inside voices.
- Eyes on me.
- Be careful.
- Be safe.

- Take your seat.
- Five more minutes.
- Use your words.

Without explanation, none of these phrases has meaning for children. Even if we have explained once or twice, children need repetition to learn. For example, "That's not polite" doesn't help Jeffrey, who just ate from the serving spoon and put it back in the bowl. Even if it's positively phrased—for example, "We need manners at the table"—the direction doesn't help Jeffrey know what the expectation is and how he can meet it. However, if a teacher says something like, "Remember, Jeffrey, the big spoon is for serving. We only use it to put food on our plate and then put it back in the bowl for others to use," she is teaching Jeffrey entry-level table manners for school lunch that he can understand. She will probably have to repeat the lesson several times before Jeffrey really grasps the concept, and he may well need more practice after that to get it right all the time, but her specific words have started the process by giving Jeffrey the clear direction he needs. It's also very important for us to say, "This is how we do it here at school," explaining that families, restaurants, cultures, countries, and lots of grannies, *mémères*, nanas, and papas have their own rules about mealtimes. We don't want to imply that the way we do things at school is the *right way*. Most of us would never say that, but most of us have sometimes implied it!

In situations like these, teachers and parents could substitute sentences like these:

- "Right now, we are in a tiny space. Let's whisper [*whisper this word*] instead of shouting."
- "Hold my hand. We are crossing the street."
- "You look sleepy, Matias. You don't need to dance. It's almost rest time."
- "You are disappointed. You wanted to run but the hall floor is still a little wet. Walk."

Teachers often assume children understand basic concepts when they don't. Three- and four-year-olds are literal thinkers. Without making too light of a very serious issue in our use of language with young children, one might envision a child thinking, *Take my seat where?* or *How do I put my eyes on her, and I don't think I want to!* Many three- and four-year-olds haven't any notion yet of "five-ness," so five more minutes or even five more orange slices is more likely to increase confusion rather than clarity.

> Young children are literal thinkers, and they need lots of time, many experiences, and probably some direct instruction to internalize what an abstract word like *nice, good, cooperative, friendly,* or *kind* means.

Many children come to us without knowing how to cut with scissors, use a glue container, pour from a pitcher, or pedal a tricycle. Teachers think of these skills at the beginning of the year when they assess children's competence. At the same time, teachers frequently assume that children know what an inside voice is or what it means to cooperate, share, clean up, wash up, or do myriad other simple tasks in daily living. To help children understand both our words and the routines in their day, we need to explain clearly what we are saying and why. "It's cleanup time" can be clarified with one more simple sentence: "That means everything needs to be put back in its place," or "Playtime is over—we need to put our things away." Repetition creates patterns. This is the way we do it at child care.

If we use a variety of sentences each week to say the same thing, we are helping children put the same meaning on a variety of words. There is a difference between using many words to provide meaning and using too many words to define a simple idea for a child. We have all heard the ancient story of the small child who got a long discussion of sex education in response to the question "Where did I come from?" when all he wanted to know was his place of birth. This is not what is being recommended here. Instead, I am suggesting that teachers be conscious of making the kind of clarifying statements that expand children's understanding of the world around them. It is then our responsibility to assess whether we have been successful at making our point. All children are different. We need to observe the children in our care, ask parents for help in familiarizing us with how toileting, eating, sleeping, and other activities are managed at home, and ask children if they understand us. Children will often be quite helpful if we ask them if we have understood them. We can't just drop a rule and expect understanding and compliance. We also cannot take that old approach that children should not be troubled with responsibilities or rules. Those of us in the rare adequately funded and staffed programs need to humble ourselves to the burdens some of our colleagues bear and not consider their rules and mode of operation developmentally inappropriate. Letting eight children meander to the bathrooms with a teacher in front and a teacher in back is quite doable; one teacher taking eighteen children to a bathroom on the next floor is quite a different adventure and needs a clear understanding of what a line is. Many programs have little opportunity to spend time with children's families. In these cases, we do the best we can. When we do reach out to parents, we can explain that we can better meet their children's needs when we know more about them. We can often accommodate parental desires when we know about them and, in doing so, help their little one be more comfortable in his days with us.

If we use a variety of sentences each week to say the same thing, we are helping children put the same meaning on a variety of words.

How does this all play out in real classrooms? Here's a story to show you from a routine visit to one of the programs I work with. I'd only been in the building a few minutes when I heard a teacher say loudly, "I need to hear silence!" I saw a puzzled look on the face of a three-year-old. I could almost hear him thinking, "How do you *hear* silence?"

I continued down the hall, pausing outside the preschool room. The teacher had gathered the children for a group time. "I'll begin the story when everyone is sitting nicely!" she said. The children continued to wiggle and squirm. The teacher became increasingly agitated. Finally, her assistant said, "C'mon, kids, we need to crisscross applesauce here." With this more specific information, most children quickly shifted to sitting with their legs crossed. However, I also noticed that two children had no idea what *crisscross applesauce* meant.

The teacher began her group time with the story *Green Eggs and Ham*. As usual, the children had comments right off the bat.

"There aren't really no green eggs."

"Are too, like you get in your Easter basket."

"Those aren't real eggs."

"Are too." (Louder.)

"No!" (Louder still.)

Here the teacher interrupted the discussion, saying, "Inside voices." The children ignored her, and her own inside voice got louder. "Inside voices!" she asserted loudly. "We need to get back to our story!" The children settled down again, but several of them were clearly still thinking about the question of green eggs and whether they really exist!

At the end of the story, the teacher asked, "What happened?"

The children said in unison, "He liked the green eggs and ham."

The teacher beamed and said, "So, you see, we should always have a no-thank-you bite, because we have to try things. We can't say we don't like something if we've never tried it." This had almost no connection whatsoever to the story.

At this point, my own inside voices were speaking to me. Here's what they said:

- Is this teacher's agenda to get the children to eat more at mealtimes?
- What is a no-thank-you bite? If you say, "No, thank you," doesn't that mean you don't want any? Why the jump to no-thank-you bites from a Seuss story the children love?
- Do the children know what the teacher means when she says "inside voices"? (I saw no evidence that they did.)

■ Why say "crisscross applesauce" if what you mean is "Sit on your bottom and cross your legs"?

Later we'll talk about the learning that was missed in this situation when the teacher didn't follow up on the children's disagreements about green eggs. For now, though, think about the difference between the directions this teacher gave the children and the behavior she wanted from them. Can you come up with more specific ways to phrase the directions? How might this story time have been different if the teacher had asked for what she wanted? What would have been the effect on the children's learning about the behavior expected of them during story time, about language, and about the content of the book?

Here's another example. What did the teacher in this story do that worked better?

Teachers in New England have a long winter to contend with. Cold and snowy weather places severe constraints on the high energy of preschoolers in programs with little indoor space for running, biking, throwing, and so on. When one fortunate program had a building addition with a large gross-motor room, the children needed time to understand how to use it!

When Kathy took her group to the room for the first time, everyone was excited. Before the children left the classroom, she had talked about safety, taking turns, and riding trikes in the same direction. When she thought the bases were covered, the group set off for the long walk down the hall, down the stairs, and into the big room. The children shrieked with excitement, raced for the trikes, and pushed and shoved. The riders who were the "fittest" were the ones who survived the mad dash! Kathy was discouraged. "Should I have waited to get downstairs before talking about safety?" she asked. "How do I do the trikes when there are only eight of them and seventeen children? The children just race for them before I get the chance to do anything!"

Kathy and I talked about the fact that her reaction to this had been one of frustration and helplessness. She did not say, "Stop right there!" or "Absolutely not!" or call the children to an immediate group time to say, "This was not our plan!" Until we talked about it, it had not occurred to her that she really hadn't done anything to redirect the group. She had assumed it was too late. As teachers, we are always able to use our adult position to change the course of events when we think it is necessary. We can stop a story time, art activity, or game and say, "This isn't working." We don't have to forge on when things are not going well simply because that was the plan. Too often we forget this. Long, long ago, John Dewey, as I recall, said something to the effect that that's why children need adults in their space! (See "My Pedagogic Creed," John Dewey's famous declaration about education first published in *The School Journal*.)

This was welcome information for this teacher. Kathy spent time thinking about entrance strategies. Her ideas were good ones. She established a rental car booth with tickets, a cash register, and even a gas pump. The rental tickets had children's names on them. The first eight were distributed at group time, upstairs. These children knew that this gave them "driving rights" as soon as they got to the gross-motor room. The addition of the gas pump, rent-a-car business, and cash register drew in the remaining children so that now the trikes were not the only point of interest. Kathy made stop signs and one-way signs and talked about following directions when you drive. With a little bit of extra effort and a whole lot of thought, she transformed a chaotic race into meaningful learning and playtime that everyone, including the teacher, was able to enjoy!

Language and Problem Solving

One of the most important jobs that is part of teaching young children is helping them make sense of the people and relationships around them, helping them learn to be with one another in groups. One way that teachers can do this is by giving children instruction and practice in talking with others about their needs and wants and solving problems together. Unfortunately, often teachers fall back on "Use your words" as an all-purpose tool. For young children who don't yet have a lot of experience with words or with relationships, this catchphrase is inadequate. It doesn't give them enough specific information to solve their problems. They don't know which words to use or how or what to do when the first set of words doesn't work. Throughout the book, we'll discuss the impact of multiple languages, ethnicity, family traditions, and ways to, hopefully, meet a majority of these needs a fair amount of the time. Again, relevant reading is included in the resources section.

Many times teachers interpret one child's hitting another as a behavior problem, when the root of the behavior is frequently confusion, frustration, or just plain not knowing what to do. When a teacher says to a child, "Is that how we treat our friends?" she is setting both the child and herself up for more confusion. Such a question violates one of the most basic guidelines for talking with young children: don't ask the question if you already know the answer. The teacher knows that pushing someone when you want her to get out of the way is not the way we treat our friends—or even people who aren't our friends. However, preschool children, relatively new to the planet, do not necessarily know this. Even if they know it in theory, they often don't know what to do instead or don't have experience with problem solving. It is our job to teach them. Teachers must take seriously the task of giving children tools for managing their day-to-day interactions with others. Also, teachers must remember the role repetition plays in learning for all of us. Once is not enough. For preschoolers, sometimes twenty times is not enough!

A better response to a child's pushing a friend out of the way might be to say something like, "Fatima, tell Adam he is in your way. Ask him to move," or "Adam, tell Fatima you don't like it when she pushes you. Ask her what she wants." This clarifies for both children that pushing isn't the answer. It gives both of them the opportunity to use language to tell others how they feel or what they need, and it offers them the specific words to use. These life skills are essential. If three-year-old Adam is in the way of three-year-old Fatima's trike, Fatima does not think that it might be seen as antisocial to shove Adam out of the way. Fatima has a goal: getting the trike (she might be learning from experience that they go fast once vacated!).

Someone needs to help her learn that we cannot just shove others out of our way when we want something, but we cannot expect children to know this before they have had instruction, practice, and repetition in ways of getting what they need or want that work in groups of children. It is also helpful to talk about this with parent groups. For many young children, school or child care is the first time they have experienced being with enough other children that there is not one of everything for everyone. Learning to wait is a teachable skill, not a developmental stage. I've often heard children discussed at parent conference time as if their parents have no desire to know what their child is really like. ("This is so hard for me to believe because she never hits at home.") It usually has not occurred to parents what their child acts like with other children. At home there might not be any other children! Children, parents, teachers, and most of us act differently at home than in public. This is important for *all* of us to remember and acknowledge.

> Children need to be taught explicitly how to use language to get what they need, and they need to be given lots and lots of practice before we should expect them to get it right.

Mistaking behavioral issues for educational ones will be discussed at length in chapter 3, but for now the lesson is that children need to be taught explicitly how to use language to get what they need, and they need to be given lots and lots of practice before we should expect them to get it right. They get taller without our help but not more socially adept.

Mandy plans and teaches at an Early Head Start socialization. This is a group that meets one day a week to provide interaction for parents and children who usually have their educational time at home. She went to her supervisor requesting additional staff because she felt the time was too chaotic. She had children ages six weeks to two years and their parents in her group. The classroom was quite large and could easily accommodate the numbers, but Mandy felt the babies were at risk because the older children were too active.

Her supervisor went to observe and found Mandy had fallen into the typical dilemma of mistaking behavioral concerns for educational ones. Mandy's planning had involved activities and materials but did not include time for working with the children to help them understand what the rules of the classroom were. Since the children were very young and came only once a week, Mandy assumed that it was not possible to teach them expectations or approaches. She was also feeling a little uncertain about directing the children when their parents were present.

Her supervisor was able to work with her on modeling adult behavior for the parents. Mandy started by talking to the toddlers, a couple at a time. She talked about babies. "Babies can't get out of our way," she said, "because they don't walk yet." She went on briefly to tell the toddlers that they were the ones who had to watch where they were going. She was surprised by how quickly the children developed a feeling of "protecting" the babies. Mandy realized that she had not been using enough language with the children. Children this young need things repeated and repeated and repeated. She continued to use "Watch for the babies" in her own language to the children on a very frequent basis. She gave more specific directions to the toddlers each time she introduced an activity, saying things like this:

- "The trikes need to stay in this part of the room. Trikes are not allowed on the rug."
- "The playdough needs to stay on the table."
- "Blocks are for building. Beanbags are for throwing."

Mandy also changed her room arrangement, using furniture to create barriers. She created sitting areas where parents and babies could be on the floor out of the way of toddler activity. All of these strategies made a huge difference to the day. It was an extra bonus for Mandy when she realized how quickly the parents had followed her lead. "Watch for the babies," parents were saying! And then one day, two-year-old Uri put his hand on eighteen-month-old Amelia's arm when she was poised to throw a beanbag. All he said was, "Baby!" There will still be times when an excited toddler steps on a baby, but the above illustrates how much growth we can nurture when we are mindful and repeat, repeat, repeat!

We always hope our approach will address both children involved in a mishap. It is so easy when a little one has been hurt for us to race over, forgetting that the child who stepped on someone is also just as surprised and scared by the crying and the situation itself. Both need our caring attention.

Asking Questions

Lack of thoughtful questioning creates many classroom problems. A very common example is using a question that implies choice when there really isn't one. We all seem to do it. Here are some examples:

- Would you like to clean that up, please?
- Would you like to go outside now?
- Would you like a no-thank-you taste?
- Would you like to share the swing now?
- Don't you think you should hold on to the handle?

In each of these cases, the adult is expecting compliance but not making that clear. We decrease frustration for children in a tough spot if we avoid using questions that imply choice when there is none. It's better to use phrases like these when there is no choice:

- Do you need some help to clean up that spilled milk?
- We are going outside now. You put on your coat, or I'll help you.
- I need to put a few green beans on your plate. If you don't want them, don't eat them.
- I'll set the timer, and when it dings, it will be time for Cal to have a turn on the swing.
- If you don't hold on to the handle, you need to get off the trampoline. I'll help you find something safe to do.

Children are confused and sometimes resentful when we use language in a way that is unclear or manipulative. Being clear when we need them to comply with a directive (and offering them real choices when we can) removes that emotional overlay and makes the job of getting through the day much easier—for all of us.

Here are some guidelines for providing clear direction and instruction as well as a couple of "clear tips":

- Be clear and specific. Don't use catchphrases or abstract concepts ("be nice") without providing explanations.

  - "Taye wants to play. You want to be alone. You can say, 'Not right now,' and take your truck over there" (pointing to an uncrowded open space).

  - "We have been having a hard time with how to do story time. We are going to try some new things. Let's try sitting on these carpet squares. Maybe that will help all of us give each other enough space to see the pages. If not, we'll try some other things." This is a perfect opportunity for children to generate ideas!

- Be concrete. Remember that children are literal thinkers.

  - If we say, "I can feel the excitement in the air" on the morning of a field trip, many little ones will look up! A better choice might be "Happy voices, busy children. We are glad to be going to the farm."

  - If we say, "Can you give him a hand?" a young child might look at her hand and say, "No—it's mine!"

- Be direct. Tell children what your expectations are simply and clearly.

  - "Start putting the balls in the bag now. We are going inside for lunch."

  - "We are going outside. Time for coats. Jenny, you need your jacket on. You can do it, or I can help you."

- Use statements, not questions, when you expect children to comply. Don't offer a choice when there isn't one.

  - Saying, "Are you ready for lunch?" will not get engaged, busy little ones to the table. Saying, "I'll hold hands with you two on the way to the table. We are going to eat now!" will.

- If we add "okay?" to an expectation, it becomes an option. Use a statement instead: "We need to pick up some of these blocks. There is no room to build."

We all require time and repetition to learn.

We are very fortunate today to have a large and helpful library of children's books that discuss, in an age-appropriate way, the many emotions we all feel as we make our way through life. It is very helpful for children to hear stories that are realistic and use simple language to attempt to soften the blow of parents divorcing, grandparents dying, making room for a new sibling, being bullied on the school bus, or moving to a new neighborhood or out in the country. Sometimes teachers have a wonderful resource library and use it only when there has been a death, a divorce, a new baby, or some other special situation. Part of our responsibility to children and their families is to regularly "teach" sadness, jealousy, fear, exuberance, shouting, and dancing and to try to weave that teaching into the day-to-day lives of children so they become aware of all of life's possibilities.

Discussion Questions

1. Why do you think teachers are so hesitant to provide children with direct instruction?

2. Share an example of a time when you gave vague instructions that resulted in an activity going poorly. What happened? What could you have done instead?

3. What are some of the things that prevent us from stating our expectations clearly? What can we do to remove some of these barriers to clear communication with children?

4. How do you handle giving directions to some children but not all? How do you respond when someone says, "How come I have to do it and she doesn't?"

5. What is your policy for sharing all of these delicate but critical curriculum areas with your families?

CHAPTER THREE

Correcting Behavior

THE MOST SOUGHT-AFTER TOPIC in early childhood education is behavior guidance. The subject is the source of book after book and technique after technique. Teachers never seem to get enough. Yet most classrooms I visit (preschool or early elementary) are still characterized by daily struggles with children's behaviors. Most teachers claim it has never been harder to manage children's daily interactions with the environment and each other. One of the things that nourishes this ever-present challenge is the tendency to mistake developmental or educational issues for behavioral problems. Too often teachers think of children as misbehaving when they are simply behaving as best they can with the information available to them.

Understanding development is critical to setting reasonable expectations for children's behaviors. Being patient is more important than we often realize. It is sometimes helpful to compare children's social-skill behaviors to their cognitive or physical behaviors. When we are reading to little ones, we don't expect them to retell the story word for word. We get excited when they learn to turn a page or recognize a familiar object in an illustration. When the baby learns to walk, we are excited by each shaky step. We are helpful and encouraging as the toddler teeters and falls again and again. Yet when it comes to hitting and biting, kicking and grabbing—the baby steps of prosocial behaviors—we get terribly impatient. We use words like *so hard*, *difficult*, and *frequent*. Few teachers would refer to a child's initial experience with paper books as "ripping too frequently," or call a child's repeated attempts at standing "difficult"! In those other areas of development, we tend to be far more patient, far less frustrated, and far less worried about a timeline. There are reasons for this, of course. Our job is to keep children safe, and hitting, kicking, biting, shoving, and grabbing put everyone at risk. But often the way we approach these challenging situations puts everyone in a riskier place than they were already in.

Accepting Authority

Lilian Katz (1977, 18) says, "Young children have to have adults who accept the authority that is theirs by virtue of their greater experience, knowledge, and wisdom. This proposition is based on the assumption that neither as parents nor as educators are we caught between the extremes of authoritarianism and permissiveness." Four decades later, it seems we are still caught in our uncertainty. Most teachers I know who are struggling with how to talk to children about behavior are full of ambivalence. They want to be effective and help children learn positive strategies for interacting, but they don't want to take charge. They don't want to accept the authority that is theirs.

I have spent a long time asking teachers where they think our hesitance comes from. This list is an array of their responses:

- We are not supposed to inhibit children's creativity.
- We need to expect two- to four-year-olds to be aggressive. It's developmental.
- I'm afraid I'll do the wrong thing.
- In college, I learned *never* to say "no" to little ones.
- I don't want to be "the mean teacher"!
- I'm not certain when I'm supposed to be directive and when I'm not.
- We all think so differently but administration does not give us time to reflect together.

Having grown up in an era when adults in general did not think that sensitivity to children's emotional needs or behavior was a priority, I have empathy for those who worry about the feelings of angry children when they can't have or do something they really want to do or believe they need. But I also believe that Dewey, long ago, and Katz, forty years ago, had it right: we are the adults. It is our responsibility to be the ones in charge. Will we make the wrong call sometimes? Of course. Will that ruin a child's life? Not likely. In an ideal world, we could all live conflict-free; we would not hit others or take their things. We would not call people names that hurt their feelings. But even though I know it's not good to yell loudly at children from across the play yard, I'll holler if it means keeping someone safe from a ball tossed too fast by an older child that could hit someone in the head from behind!

In a 2014 article in *The Nation*, Mychal Denzel Smith outlined points made in recent years in many disciplines. These articles involve the reports of the US Department of Education Office for Civil Rights that have been discussed in many different arenas regarding the disproportionate number of black and male students expelled from preschools in the United States. They also bring attention to the fact that female students are often expelled for being too loud, even if they are not specifically violating school rules and regulations. When these articles initially received public attention, there was a sense of shock that somehow children so young could be expelled for behavioral reasons. We have already discussed that it is generally accepted that preschool is the place where children learn these expectations. How then, we ask ourselves, can they be expelled for not already knowing these expectations and abiding by them when they are not yet five years old?

I am taking a bold step here in stating that the public preschool teachers, and even primary teachers, who don't know what to do with these behaviors often do not know because they have not been adequately educated in child growth and development. (I have always felt a little more daring than some of my colleagues in talking about elementary education certification rather than ECE certification because—long ago!—I was certified in both.) I have observed ECE graduates manage seven languages, nine individualized education programs (IEPs), and state guidelines that are not a good match for developmentally appropriate guidelines in a class of twenty-two students with no aide, and they still manage to make children feel safe. Knowing what to expect from children does not make their demanding, inconvenient, urgent, or physical needs easier to meet. However, teachers who know this is how four-year-olds are have a leg up on colleagues trained solely in pedagogical methods with only Human Development and Learning and Introduction to Psychology to fall back on when the *reality* of a day in preschool presents itself. I believe that both early educators and primary educators feel the pain of this situation and wish it were different. Many ECE-trained teachers have admitted to me that they feel belittled when they enter primary schools because they are judged as unprepared to teach. At the same time, many elementary teachers admit that they feel they don't know what to do about behavior guidance with their children and envy the ECE-trained teachers.

Clearly, to say that the expulsion and suspension challenges we face are as simple as which teacher preparation course should be accepted where is not the answer. It may, however, be a key to some progress that we have been overlooking. When I serve on Department of Education committees for my own state of New Hampshire, I am always amazed when I speak with area superintendents who are surprised or even incredulous that there are four- and five-year-olds being suspended and expelled. They say it is difficult to hire ECE graduates because they cannot be easily moved throughout the system when there is turnover. These same administrators admit that it is hard to keep teachers in the pre-k through grade three age group. Though many admitted that formal exit interviews were not being conducted, most teachers who left said informally that the children were "just too hard." Yet teachers in the primary grades whose degrees are in early childhood education (all say, "Don't quote me") are frequently told by colleagues, "Every year you get the easy kids!" In reality, it is simply that the teacher knows how to teach these children. She understands child development and knows how to manage the spectrum of behaviors young children exhibit. The fact is that colleagues without early-childhood-specific education do not always understand the connection between their colleague's training and the children's more positive behaviors. This is so sad for everyone. It is not only conventional wisdom, at this point, but is well documented by years of research, that if teachers know child development and developmentally appropriate curriculum, the work becomes easier for all involved and the outcomes for children and families are brighter.

We should all take our responsibility, as adults, to think before we speak if we have the time to ponder the situation and our choice of words. Sometimes we have neither. We need to do the best we can. Then we can return when things settle and say to a child, "I hope I didn't scare you when I yelled so loudly, but I was afraid you might be hit. I needed to keep you safe." Keeping children safe is not being the mean teacher. Children rely on us to help them meet our expectations. In rare situations, that can mean really raising our voices. Further, when that startling pitch and loudness are rare, children tend to respond almost instinctively to our voice. If yelling is what we do all day every day, regardless of the age of the child, it just becomes more of the "blah, blah, blah" we all hear too much of.

Over the years, I have heard Dr. Lilian Katz refer to *analysis paralysis*. As I recall, she used this phrase to refer to both parents and teachers. Though she congratulated us all for wanting to do well by children, she urged us to also accept that there is a time when pondering is overdone and one needs to take action—even if, in retrospect, a better choice could have been made.

I've heard T. Berry Brazelton say many times that in his decades of working with infants, children, and families, parents often left his conferences treasuring the most surprising fact: they were not alone. By that he meant that they were not alone in having children who screamed, spit, kicked, wailed, grabbed, hit, and threw things. The reality for many young families is that they are very much alone in their daily struggles with behaviors that they just don't know how to handle. My conversations with preschool, kindergarten, and primary-grade teachers tell me that early educators are feeling pretty much the same way. Let's look in on one of these educators as she struggles with umbrellas:

It was late March in New Hampshire when I visited Corinne's classroom. Teachers had gathered umbrellas for use under the melting icicles along the edges of the building. Children wore rain jackets and boots and were enjoying the melting of snow and ice. During a twenty-five-minute outdoor playtime, it did not take long for problems like running with umbrellas, climbing with umbrellas, and using umbrellas as weapons to surface. Corinne's dilemma was complicated because she had not given specific directions and boundaries for the use of the umbrellas prior to using them. During that brief period of time, I heard her tell Hayley four times, "Umbrellas are not allowed on the climbing structure." This statement was ignored four times by Hayley, who might not have had any idea that Corinne was trying to tell her to get down because she didn't actually tell her that!

What exactly were the problems here?

- Corinne did not give specific directions for use of the materials *in advance*.

- She was not at all clear in her expectations. (For example, saying that umbrellas cannot go up a climbing structure is unclear to children.)

- Corinne delivered an opinion and thought she had given a directive. (A directive would have been: "Get down. That's not safe.")

- Corinne did not keep children safe. (Hayley was in a dangerous position, and Corinne should have stopped it with a statement like "You may climb *or* play with the umbrella but not both. You make a choice, or I'll need to help you.")

- Corinne did not follow through to remove Hayley from the climbing structure. She kept saying, "Umbrellas are not allowed on the climbing structure," but she allowed Hayley to continue playing on it.

A related point to remember here is that if you give a child a directive several times and the child finally follows it, saying "Good job getting down!" is not appropriate. Ignoring directions four or five times is not doing a good job. The teacher's responsibility is to say things clearly and then follow through with action. If you say "get down" and the child ignores you, take her off the climbing structure. Hold her hand, smile, show her that if she holds the umbrella upside down it can be like a bucket that col-

> The teacher's responsibility is to say things clearly and then follow through with action.

lects water or spun like a top if it is small enough. She is then aware that you are not angry with her because she did not get down, but she knows you will keep her safe.

When Corinne and I met after this discouraging morning, she knew she had been ineffective with Hayley. She said something that left me feeling discouraged and concerned about ineffective teacher preparation. "If you had not been observing, I would have taken her off the structure, but I thought you would think I was being authoritarian!" The root of her comment is the common notion that being authoritative and direct is somehow being authoritarian. My work with teachers tells me this is a widespread challenge to our discipline. I agree with Lilian Katz that we need to work on accepting the authority that is ours. Children are left confused or, as in Hayley's case, at risk when we do not provide the adult supervision and directives necessary to keep them informed and safe—whether they like it or not.

Then we need to be prepared for tears, stomping, or some expression of anger. For decades parents (and sometimes even teachers) said things like, "Stop that right now" to something as simple as hopping on one foot while standing in line, followed by, "And wipe that look off your face!" Usually the harsher "Stop that crying or I'll give you something to cry about" was reserved for inside the house. In other words, children were told both to stop doing something that they liked or something that offered them fun or comfort and then to act like it was okay with them to stop. It is progress that, at least in theory, we expect children to be miffed if we ask them to stop. But when safety is the situation, it is our job to do so. The story of Laurie below shows us the positive value of setting limits and enforcing them consistently.

Here is an example of a teacher who accepts her authority with young children without being authoritarian or punitive. Laurie's room backs up to a field, woods, and then the community elementary school. This wonderful arrangement provides a safe and rich outdoor learning environment for her four-year-olds. Laurie is sensitive to young children's need for running and independence. Her particular location allows her to provide more of this than many of us are fortunate enough to have. She has an agreement with the elementary school to use its playground when the school's students are not outside. Laurie has mapped with photographs the route through the field and woods to the school. There are several big markers along the way—a huge rock, a fallen tree, a big stump, and so forth. Before her outings, she goes over the map at group time and tells children they may run ahead until they get to the big stump. "When everyone reaches it, you may run to the huge rock," she says, reminding them that everyone needs a partner and no one may run ahead alone. She is very clear. They work independently *and* as a group as they reach each marker.

On the day I took this trip with them, Ramone broke the rules. He ran ahead by himself, though he stopped at the designated marker. When Laurie had the whole group together at the first marker, she said clearly, "Ramone, I'm disappointed that you did not stay with Micco. Everyone *must* have a partner." Her tone and facial expression were sober. Her expectations were clear. She gave Ramone another chance but also stated the consequences, *in advance*, should he not stay with Micco to the next marker. "If you do not stay with Micco, I'll need to be your partner for the rest of the trip," she said. The race was on. The children took off, and once again Ramone left Micco behind. At the huge rock, Laurie collected the group and took Ramone firmly by the hand. She didn't say a word. She announced the next marker, the children ran off, and she kept Ramone firmly at her side. He squirmed, frowned, cried, and then accepted his fate. Laurie smiled at him and picked up her pace. They ran together, laughing and racing. The few minutes of Ramone's struggle for independence he could not handle was a small price to pay for the assurance he felt as he ran with his teacher: the certainty that she would keep him safe helped him to do what needed to be done. This is a wonderful gift that strong teachers give to the children in their care.

Behind Behavior: Four Factors

The way we talk to children in situations involving inappropriate behavior is an area in need of much discussion and clarification. This is complex because the problem is multidimensional. I think Gwen Morgan's (2001) statements about complicated and complex bear repeating here. There are no simple answers. The best we can hope for is a toolkit of assorted coping strategies to help children live and learn in a complex world. In thinking about the problem of "teacher talk" with children in behavior management situations, we have to consider these four pieces of the picture:

- teachers
- parents
- children
- context

TEACHERS

Discussing discipline and young children is a delicate issue in the early childhood field. All one has to do is listen to teachers participating in a workshop on the topic to verify this. "I prefer *not* to say the word *discipline*!" someone will say with passion. "It's so punitive! I prefer *guidance*!" Heads will nod in approval, and teachers immediately zoom off on the topic of positive language, rephrasing the negative to give children an idea of what *to* do instead of what not to do.

Though I used to encourage teachers years ago to find ways to phrase most of their directives to children in the positive, I have stopped. I think we've gone too far. We don't like to talk about it much, but all the while that teachers are saying they don't even want to say the word *discipline*, they are claiming that children's behavior

We don't like to talk about it much, but all the while that teachers are saying they don't even want to say the word *discipline*, they are claiming that children's behavior has never been more difficult.

has never been more difficult. When children get nothing but sweet smiles and vague comments about not hitting our friends in child care, it's no wonder chaos reigns in many programs. I've been trying to empower teachers lately to give a good firm "Stop!" with a frown on their face when a child is about to hurt another. Recently a colleague shared another powerful deterrent with me: "Absolutely not!" a teacher might say with an "I mean business" look on her face. Don't be afraid to accept the authority that is yours. Find your voice so you can help children find theirs!

Many textbooks offer us checklists on children's behavior aimed at assisting us in identifying our own weak points, sometimes referred to as *flash points*. We all have vulnerabilities to certain behaviors. Often our flash points are connected to our own upbringing or early school years. These flash points are the things that make us really cringe when colleagues observing the same behavior have no problem at all. It may be whining, shouting, swearing, tattling, or hitting. Years ago, when I was teaching Guiding Behavior courses, parents in my class wanted to know what to do to make the children behave. I would say, "I'm not sure!" I would urge them to discuss with each other what the biggest challenges were and how they coped. Usually an articulate, outspoken person would speak for the group and say, "That's why we took the course. You are supposed to tell us the right way to handle it!" It was always a sad and poignant moment when I had to say, "It depends." One parent said her oldest always grabbed things from her youngest, and she didn't know what to do. He was bigger and could always get what he wanted by grabbing. "So, you don't want him to grab?" I would ask. "What if you taught him to yell loudly, 'It's mine—get the hell away from me!'?" Silence would fall over the classroom. It was the '70s! After moments of shocked silence, the group speaker would say, "Well we don't want him to swear either." I would hear the murmurs of approval. Then I would use the greenboard, writing the following: Problem: two-and-a-half-year-old grabs toy from six-month-old and always wins. Possible solutions:

- This is America! Might makes right, correct? (Class votes no!)
- Teach older child to swear, scaring younger sibling who will then retreat. (Class votes no!)
- Take all toys away from both boys and watch TV. (Class votes no!)

I will not bore you with the many responses from five years of teaching the same course. I will summarize. By the end of the course most students, year after year, agreed on the following:

- They didn't want children to be angry, sad, or mad.
- They wanted the children to behave!
- They felt incompetent when their children hit, bit, or acted out (whatever that means to whom!).
- It had never occurred to them that children had all these feelings and didn't know what to do with them.
- They were all greatly affected by what other parents, other teachers, their in-laws, and total strangers in the supermarket thought of them.
- They deeply loved their children and wanted to do a good job but didn't know what that really meant.

We may not quite know why, but whenever questionable (according to whom?) behavior surfaces in our classroom, our ability to cope feels diminished. This is absolutely normal and common to all people who work with children. One thing that often helps is to identify what your own flash points are. When you know you have a vulnerability to whining, and you know Heather frequently whines in response to things like change, discomfort, and interruption, it's a good idea to let your assistant or colleague manage Heather on a day that you already have a headache. One of the most helpful solutions to this dilemma is teacher reflection. Margie Carter and Deb Curtis (1994) make the point that we go from task to task in our work, sometimes not taking the time to discuss how things went or *felt*. Reflection with colleagues can really be a support when dealing with children's difficult behaviors and our own difficult reactions to them.

It is a financial reality of some federally funded programs, or their leadership, that reflecting as teachers or social workers on the challenges of daily life in our programs is viewed as a waste of time or of taxpayers' dollars. In these times of reduced budgets when supportive reflection with colleagues may be most of what we have left to use to support children and families well, we may need to rethink our priorities. (Read *Training Teachers* by Deb Curtis and Margie Carter to learn more about the importance of reflection.) It is not a luxury for staff to discuss case studies, behavior, and their own personal reactions to those things. Rather, it is a critical component of doing our best job to support children, their families, and our own professional growth and development.

PARENTS

In 1999 Rebecca New shared with teachers her experiences working with families in Italy in a lecture to Strafford County Head Start. In her experience, the parent dimension in Italy is often not quite so complicated as it gets here because the culture is more homogeneous. Parents, teachers, and grandparents have greater agreement regarding what is good for children. Most teachers I talk to struggle with the fact that parents of the children they care for want very different things for their children. Some parents, teachers tell me, do not want their children corrected by anyone. These parents feel their children are too young to understand limits and will be stifled by teacher direction. In the same class are parents who arrive in September offering a wooden spoon and requesting that teachers use it on the child's legs if she misbehaves. Some parents don't want male children wearing dress-up clothes, some don't want their children to get their clothes dirty, and some want teachers to teach their three-year-olds to read. There are parents who expect you to prevent biting in a toddler room and parents who want you to bite a child back when he bites!

So, what is a teacher to do? Our first professional response is to remember that these families all love their children and want to do well by them. They do not want their children to hit, spit, or hurt others, but they don't know how to prevent these behaviors. In recent years, researchers have concluded that the "push-down" curriculum most primary and kindergarten teachers are dealing with has only made behavioral challenges worse. When families want their children to have a better chance in life than they have had, it makes sense for them to believe learning to read might be one of the keys to that goal. It is not their job to know that rote teaching of letters and sounds, out of context, will not accomplish early reading expertise. That is our job as early childhood educators. It is also our job, over time, to show parents how children learn so many wonderful things (eventually— including prereading competence) through the many individual and group activities they explore throughout their days and early years with us.

Years ago, the answer to this question was always "Educate the parents!" We have learned a great deal over the years, and now most teachers agree it isn't quite that simple. As we have done more cross-discipline work, we have learned that we need to consider health, socioeconomic factors, cultural, family, regional, and other individual differences between teachers and the families they work with. Equally important to such critical factors listed above are temperament (of teachers, children, and parents), personalities, individual interests, and learning styles. Teachers' jobs are not so simple as educating parents, children, colleagues, or school boards in the right ways! Yes, there are some incorrect approaches, but there are many, many appropriate approaches to helping individual children and families move forward. The challenge is in having the time, patience, support, and information that will give us a better chance at matching the approach to the child and family. To do right by children, teachers have to be as open to learning from the parents as we want them to be open to learning from us. Parental expectations differ as we move from one socioeconomic or cultural group to the next (Wardle 1999) and one family to the next, yet many teachers and programs don't modify their expectations or delivery to accommodate these differences. Again, I cautiously urge a mindful approach to this dilemma.

In the United States, we are not allowed to administer physical discipline to stop challenging behavior, at least not in most schools and programs. Many of us totally endorse this policy and can find a strong but nonjudgmental voice in stressing to parents that we cannot and will not punish children in response to their behaviors. We need to be careful that we don't fall back into the old "I'm the teacher and I know best" attitude. Initially, it is not helpful to introduce a brand-new concept to parents by accompanying it with written brochures (often not in their language) or phone numbers of agencies that might offer more information.

As stated above, this is long, slow, important work. In an age where so many of us look for immediacy in every aspect of our lives, teachers and parents who want this solved *right now* are likely to be bitterly disappointed. Revisit the discussion above about slowing down. Addressing these issues can only enhance our ability to meet the needs of more children and create more peaceful classrooms. But it takes group vision, commitment, great tolerance for ambivalence and imperfection, patience, trying, and trying again. It takes the courage to carefully plan and then realize the carefully thought-out plan is not working so we need to go back to the drawing board!

We can start by taking a look at our personal and program approach to challenging behaviors and sharing solutions and problem solving with parents in the process of creating a variety of responses. We can also create a vision statement or agency commitment to the fact that this processing and reflective dialogue is not a waste of time or taxpayers' dollars but the only way to humanistically view and consider the many diverse challenges we all bring to the table.

We have previously discussed ethnocentrism in approaching children and families. It is an understandable fact of life that we tend to enter the adult world or community thinking that the way we were taught to do things or the way we experienced them is "the way" those things are or should be done. Realizing that our way is one of uncountable ways things can be done is humbling.

Here are some examples of ethnocentrism often heard in early childhood settings:

- She's way too young to consider toilet teaching.

- It's time to get her on a bottle (or using a cup).

- He should be sleeping in his own bed.

- We need to get her to speak up when she needs something.

- That's not the kind of word nice people use.

- You need to get Nana to understand how important independence is.

- Tell her to tell his *pépère* to make him use a fork. It's embarrassing for a child that age to be fed by an adult.

Long ago most early educators abandoned expressions like *good girl*, *bad boy*, *stupid*, *naughty*, and so on. Less than a month ago, however, I overheard a teacher say, "That's a nasty word," in response to a four-year-old's use of the *F*-word. Think about the unspoken judgment this phrase implies of a child's uncle, mother, or sibling who might use the *F*-word frequently. A phrase like "That's a word we don't use at school" is more effective because it is not value-laden. It informs the child about the school's expectation without judging her family.

I feel like I could be accused of speaking out of both sides of my mouth on this one. But, although being genuine is important, so is accepting the changes in the last fifty years of how we define *family*. All families are unique. Regardless of the country we come from; the religion we practice, or don't; the politics we prefer; how we spend our leisure time (if we are fortunate enough to have any); what foods we like, or don't; what makes us laugh, or not; our dreams for our children; our hopes for the future—we all have all of those things.

Whether or not we use the *F*-word at home should not be part of our professional analysis of the stability or quality of care a child is receiving. For many of us, this is a real struggle. Some of us have been brought up with the idea that some things are acceptable and others are not. This is one of those dilemmas where I continually disappoint students who are seeking answers about what exactly to do. But as referenced above, the world is changing. What children hear at home and on TV makes it impossible for us to be the judge of what language is "acceptable." We can, at best, suggest guidelines for our classroom communities.

I frequently repeat that Gwen Morgan of Wheelock College (2001) has given us the thoughtful challenge of differentiating the things that are complex in our work from those that are complicated. The complicated can be simplified, but the complex can only be coped with. Morgan claims we have put misdirected energy into trying to simplify the complex, when our task is to develop coping strategies for complexity and a greater tolerance for ambiguity—for the many times in working with children and families when there is no "right" way. At this extremely pivotal time in our nation's history, many of us wonder what the future holds for us, for our children, for our grandchildren. We can model for the next generation if we have the courage, the fortitude, and the self-discipline to be respectful, try not to hurt each other, and be open to many ways to get to a goal.

CHILDREN

When we create a plan for classroom management, we need to begin with observation. As with curriculum, our approach to guiding behavior must be individualized. This creates distress for many teachers I know. Teachers love the word *consistency*, and nowhere is it more consistently applied than the area of child guidance. Yet individual children have different temperaments, personalities, and developmental needs. The same behavior does not necessarily mean the same thing when it is engaged in by different children. Teachers are the adults. Rules in a program need to be few but well maintained. Therefore, a great rule for places where young children spend their days is "Listen to the teacher in your room" or "Listen to the grown-up in charge." That way the safety of the environment can be established by children understanding that we are there to support them and keep them safe. They can cope with adults having different interpretations of a rule. Children manage this at home with their parents, grandparents, and other adults. They can do it at school too. But they will be able to do it at school only when we develop a greater tolerance for ambivalence and more confidence in making decisions on behalf of the children in our care. We need to continue to work on our inability to accept ambivalence as a natural part of responsible decision making. It is not always possible to feel completely comfortable with our decisions or course of action. But we must act.

Some of this hesitation comes from the extent to which positive guidance has been confused with permissiveness. A majority of the discipline mistakes made by teachers of children under the age of five has to do with a lack of knowledge of child growth and development. Recently I read an updated piece that quoted Marcy Whitebook (Nadworny 2016) and colleagues stating that just over 50 percent of teachers in the ECE workforce now have degrees in preparation for doing this most important work. Conventional wisdom and workers with twenty years of experience or more (remember, we can sometimes have twenty years of experience at doing something poorly) frequently say they'd prefer someone with experience who likes children over one of those college students who thinks he knows everything! I prefer the college-educated, ECE-trained teachers who like children and realize they will never know everything. I have visited centers where a toddler teacher who doesn't even know me says things like the following:

- "Watch out for that one—she's a bully." Her coworkers vigorously nod in approval.

- "We wanted to get rid of that one—he's a biter! But the director says we need his tuition. Two really great kids with good parents have left because of that biter."

- "You can see this is just not working. We could use some help."

I agreed with her. They did need help understanding typical toddler behavior. I cannot hold caregivers responsible for repeating well-worn old wives tales or conventional wisdom suggesting children are born wild and need to be tamed by adult ideas. But I can hold responsible those of us who have been fortunate enough to learn more responsive ways to care for and teach the very young, founded on evidence-based practices. We are responsible for speaking out about the necessity of all teachers being required to learn about and follow these well-documented approaches to supporting children and their families. Teachers need to understand that temperament affects all humans. Some of us are docile. Some of us are not. We all can change and grow, and we need support and guidance to do so.

Recently a teacher explained to me that in her classroom they were struggling with transitions and had set firmer limits around mealtime routines. It was only the third day of new routines when I visited the classroom. I sat next to a little boy who was told he needed to stay in his seat until his friends had finished eating. He had eaten quickly and wanted to return to a project, but the new routines included staying at the table until most of the children were done. He asked several times if he could get up. The teacher was struggling and finally said, "I'm so sorry I have to make you stay here, but it's the new rule."

After the children had gone, we talked about this incident. The teacher said she felt that she was being mean to the little boy. She said she wanted to let him do what he wanted to do because that was what she had learned in college about being responsive to young children. Most of us could agree that children behave better when we reduce waiting in our routines. However, for the child to have an apology from a teacher because she was carrying out a new plan (agreed on by faculty) for smoother mealtime routines does not help him learn about life or waiting. More important, it doesn't help him trust that his teacher knows how to meet his needs with confidence.

Frederick Buechner (2007, 209) has said that the main job of a teacher "is to teach gently the inevitability of pain." Sometimes it is helpful if teachers use words like "right now." I don't mean this in the context of telling a three-year-old to "clean this space right now." But it is helpful if children can gradually learn that just because we can't do something we want to today, it doesn't necessarily mean we can never do it. In my many years of working in the field, I've found that the word *consistency* is the one most used by all teachers to justify rules. Again, Katz and Chard (1989) state that we overestimate children developmentally while underestimating them cognitively. The idea that a staff of forty in a building will never agree on all rules for the use of a slide is probably something we could all agree on. However, the children in their care can truly understand a response of "It's fine if Heather lets you do that, but right now I'm the adult in charge and, to me, it doesn't feel safe."

Returning to the example of the little boy at the lunch table and his teacher who apologized for following through on a new staff-approved policy, how could this teacher have handled the situation more positively? Knowing that the new rule required children to wait at the table until most of them were done eating, teachers in the room might have been prepared to help children with the task of waiting. Engaging children in interesting conversations or playing a game of I Spy, for instance, would have supported the children's learning of a new skill. One thing children don't need from us is a public display of the fact that we are anxious about being the grown-up who needs to know how to manage our day-to-day adventures and routines with confidence. It is okay to say, "We are trying this out." It is okay to say, "This may not work." It is okay to say, "We'll see." It is okay to say, "This is not working." Then we can reflect, observe, listen, think, communicate, and come up with a better approach—because we are the teachers, right now, who are in charge of making the decision. It is our professional responsibility. The children are counting on us. It's also true that if the teacher knew this little one had really had enough, she could have quietly said, "Go on—finish your project." Probably more than half of the other children would not have noticed. If someone did and questioned her, she could have said, "Yes, he did leave the table. I decided he needed to get back to his work." We get so afraid anarchy will break out if we bend the rules. Another great example is "It's cold out—everyone needs to wear a sweater." Teachers have said to me for decades, "If we let one child take off her sweater, everyone else will do it too!" That may be true, but if children are allowed to measure their own comfort level, they'll put it right back on if they feel cold. If anarchy breaks out for seven minutes, it will be forgotten by the end of the day!

CONTEXT

In an abstract of Urie Bronfenbrenner's 1970 publication, *Two Worlds of Childhood: U.S. and U.S.S.R.*, Julius Richmond (American Psychological Association 2004) refers to Bronfenbrenner as one of the distinguished social psychologists of our times. He describes Bronfenbrenner's central research question as "How can we judge the worth of a society?" When Bronfenbrenner died a dozen years ago, he was still pursuing information on that primary question. Though he is not always included as key to ECE in academic programs, he became a key part of my continued work in the field because he was the first to look at child development in context. Discussion of his work and contributions demand volumes, but in brief, he was a developmental psychologist, a founding father of Head Start, and a professor for decades in Human Development and Family Studies and Psychology at Cornell University. Equally as important, he was the father of six children and a lifelong learner.

The reason for inserting this section on context in a book about how our verbal communication, or lack thereof, affects children's learning is that Bronfenbrenner's years of study (including years of cross-cultural and group work as well as his individual work) came up with a direct answer to his primary research question: how do we judge the worth of a society? It is an answer that includes many of the factors of current research (for example, race, ethnicity, poverty, gender, stereotyping, education, housing, population, violence) on what we should do in the United States and around the world. His answer? Our worth as a society and our projections of future success or demise depend on the level of concern we have *today* for how our decisions, policies, actions, and day-to-day living will affect the next generation and generations to come.

In North America, our approach to many developmental issues, such as feeding, weaning, toileting, and sleeping arrangements, have been pretty ethnocentric over the years. As we ponder the many variables that make our work guiding the behavior of young children complex, we must consider context. Many of us, particularly white, middle-class women, feel uncomfortable approaching the topic of cultural differences. We have much work to do. Considering these powerful factors should have an impact on approaches we take in our daily work with children. Yet frequently we are judgmental regarding parenting practices that are different from ours, and both children and their parents know it. We need to broaden our definitions of guidance. We need to learn more about each other. We need to address our discomforts with all the newness of trying to interpret our work in a more global way.

Despite hours of research in preparation for revising this book, I think the most timely and honest suggestion for approaching some of the dilemmas we face using words with children in a too-rapidly changing world came to me while relaxing! In recent years, comedians have done much to poke fun at themselves and their ethnic, racial, and socioeconomic groups. While relaxing recently, I heard comedian Hasan Minhaj (Gajanan 2017) referencing media and language wars in the United States as citizens with differing opinions on many important issues continue to battle while on screen and, thus, in front of both young children and the rest of the world. He suggested to the press that they needed to learn to think, act, and feel some of the pressure minorities face all of their lives:

> You gotta be on your A-game. You gotta be twice as good. You can't make any mistakes. Because when one of you messes up, he blames your entire group. And now you know what it feels like to be a minority. [. . .] And now that you're a minority [. . .] everyone is going to expect you to be a mouthpiece for the entire group. [. . .] See now that you are truly a minority, there's a distorted version of you out there. You know, Taco Bell for Mexican culture. Panda Express for Chinese culture. [. . .] And then, when you actually manage to do great work, you get hit with the most condescending line in the English language: "Hey, you're actually one of the good ones."

In using the above reference, I do not intend to make light of a very serious challenge to our daily work with children, families, and each other. Nor do I suggest that we should just accept that things are hard and do the best we can without searching for innovative and creative solutions to all of this. It is my hope that I am stressing that human needs have always been complex, always been conflicting in one way or another, and that the answers are not simple, immediate, or permanent.

Jumping from humor to the very serious *Journal of Linguistic Anthropology*, I found this statement by Shirley Brice-Heath (2015) both accurate and encouraging: "Academic research alone cannot alter economic realities or political will. What scholars in linguistic anthropology and other fields willing to take up a long-term perspective *can* do is insistently push against searches for simple solutions." I believe that is a direction in which early childhood educators are well positioned to move.

Teachers who work with diverse families (in other words, all teachers and all families) must be informed about and comfortable with a variety of approaches to discipline. Saying "children of color" or "poverty" may be a perfect choice of words for the situation or context. But we also need to remember we are making generalizations that are as invalid in some contexts as they are valid in others. However we each view what is best for coming generations, there are many general approaches we can take in our work. Below is a partial list of ideas concerning diversity generated from both students of ECE and veteran teachers of children from birth through grade three:

- Different families and cultures do not always share the same idea of what is safe space and supervision for young children.

- We need to learn more about the cultures of families who are new to our country and help them learn more about ours.

- This work is very time consuming and important, and it doesn't produce immediate results.

- While American educators tend to view TV as a deterrent to learning, many refugee and immigrant families view it as a language teacher.

- Most teachers need to develop more skill at viewing scenarios from different angles.

- Most teachers need to reflect on the extent to which we have been conditioned to be ethnocentric.

- We need to work on accepting many ways of accomplishing the same goal.

- We need to work on having respectful disagreements and accepting, in practice, that consistency in some situations is critical and in other situations is irrelevant.

Teacher Talk and Behavior Guidance

So, what does all of this mean when teachers are actually in the classroom with children? There is probably no situation in which clear teacher talk is more necessary than in the area of child guidance. Discipline situations require many things simultaneously from teachers:

- the ability to move quickly

- the ability to be fair

- the ability to keep children safe physically and emotionally

- the understanding that we are teaching everyone in the room, because they'll all be watching

- the ability to offer alternatives to inappropriate choices

To see how clear teacher talk can help with all of this, let's look at it in practice. Here's an example of a behavior guidance moment in a kindergarten classroom. Three boys were bouncing on a sofa that had been foolishly placed in front of a large window. The teacher clearly wanted this to stop but was ambivalent about how to get that to happen.

"I'm concerned that someone will be hurt," she said sweetly with a pleasant smile on her face. Not surprisingly, the boys ignored her.

Her second attempt was a little stronger. "This looks dangerous to me," she said, not smiling. The boys continued to bounce.

Her third attempt sounded frustrated and angry. "You boys need to make other choices, *now!*" she said loudly. The boys, who were quite fond of this teacher, looked confused and hurt. They got down from the sofa and wandered around the room. They did not seem sure of what they had done but were clearly affected by their teacher's displeasure.

After class the teacher talked with me about her frustration with the lack of discipline in her class. "The children don't listen to me. I don't know what to do," she said. We talked about the bouncing boys. She truly thought she had given them clear directions. We talked about the difference between an opinion ("I'm concerned") and a directive ("Please get down now. That's not safe").

We also talked about trying to match tone of voice, body language, and facial expression to the situation. It had not occurred to her that her smile and gentle tone prevented the children from hearing her concern. When we have a serious message to deliver to children, we must do so in a serious tone of voice. Perhaps a frown is also in order. Safety is important. Children will not understand a serious warning if it is given in a gentle voice with a sweet smile. It is likewise important to shift gears once the dangerous behavior has ended. The above teacher could have given a firm directive followed by a softer voice, a smile, and a suggestion. "You boys need to bounce. Let's find the trampoline—and remember, sofas are for sitting!"

Let's think about the four components of behavior guidance as they affect this scenario of bouncing boys: moving quickly, being fair, keeping children safe, teaching everyone in the room, and offering alternatives. How could the teacher feel successful in such a situation considering all of these?

- She could have gone right to the sofa and assisted the boys in finding a safer place to bounce. She might have said, "Please get down now. This is not safe." (moving quickly, keeping children physically safe)

- She could use clear statements, use a firm tone of voice, and not smile when addressing unsafe behavior. (being fair)

- By putting an end to dangerous behavior in a fair way and by asserting her authority, she would provide clarity about what was acceptable and reassure children that she was strong enough to keep them safe. (teaching everyone, keeping children emotionally safe)

- She could have acknowledged the boys' need to bounce and found a way for them to do so safely. (offering alternatives)

Using Clear Language

Like other areas of teacher talk, our behavioral interventions with children are often directed by vague and uncertain words, fads, or poorly matched words and body language or tone of voice. Our best intentions combined with the above pitfalls result in our using expressions that baffle children completely and teach them little or nothing. Here are a few examples:

- "We don't hit (kick, bite, push) our friends in child care"—when somebody just did!

- "Tell her you're sorry. We don't hurt our friends"—when children are not sorry and they have hurt someone!

- "The sand needs to stay in the box"—as if sand had free will and is not being thrown by a person!

Teachers also often ask questions that don't clarify the situation but instead further confuse or put on the spot children who are already upset. For example, here are a couple of questions that are not usually helpful:

- "Who had it first?" The response to this one is usually "I did" in unison! For children who are often still operating by the toddler's rules of possession ("If I saw it first, it's mine"), this question is irrelevant.

- "How would you like it if she did that to you?" Preschool-age children are not too young for empathy, but they are too young for a hypothetical situation like this one, especially when the reality is exactly the opposite. It is better to clearly state the other child's feelings and to help the child who has inadvertently hurt another in order to get what she needs herself, to tune in to visual cues about others' reactions: "That hurt Desmond. Look, he's crying."

The initial intent of such vague language was to prevent the kind of damaging words adults used many years ago with children. Avoiding name-calling like *bad*, *nasty*, and *unkind* is a worthy and appropriate goal. But to say, "We don't hit" right in the midst of one child hitting another is confusing. "Stop. You're hurting Omar!" helps a child know what you want her to do and why. The third and critical piece of this kind of behavioral intervention is telling the child what *to do* instead.

1. "Stop." (what needs to be done)

2. "You're hurting Omar." (why it needs to be done)

3. "Tell him you're still using the trike." (giving the child the actual alternative to pushing or hitting and the words to use as well)

Remembering that this kind of teaching involves continual repetition and patience is vital. Helping children learn self-control and social skills takes a very long time and much practice. When teachers respond to children's physical behaviors with each other in the same teaching way that they respond to other developmental milestones, children eventually learn the whole lesson we want them to learn: we can't hurt each other. We need to use words to get what we need and tell others how we feel. It is an exciting moment for a teacher who has said over and over again, "I can't let you hit. Hitting hurts. Use your words instead. Tell her to leave you alone," to watch a child, block in hand, ready to strike, *consciously* stop and say, "Go away. I want to be alone!"

Getting to that day, however, is a long journey that takes patience, skill, and understanding. We need to develop empathy for the intense feelings young children have when they have not yet learned how to manage socially. In *Listen to the Children* (Zavitkovsky, Baker, et al. 1986), these feelings are described perfectly:

Kevin and Greg are building blocks together. Kevin gets angry because Greg takes a block from him. They fight. The teacher intervenes and talks with Kevin about using words instead of fists. She tells him to try talking to Greg instead of hitting him—to tell Greg what was making him angry. Finally believing she has made her point, she asks Kevin, "Now what would you like to do?" Kevin answers without hesitation, "Hit him!" and he does!

The teacher was hoping (as we so often do!) for the response "Say I'm sorry." But note the language she used: "What would you like to do?" The child's response to this question was honest. Perhaps it was the wrong question—or perhaps what was needed at that point was not a question at all. We need to remember that heartfelt, sincere apologies in times of stress on a preschool floor are as likely as children stating, "This puzzle is beyond my developmental abilities," rather than pitching it angrily when they can't make the pieces fit. Haim Ginott (1965) was among the first to say out loud that when adults coerce an apology from young children, they are, indeed, teaching them to tell their first lies! Young children push, hit, and grab at each other because they are still learning how to get what they need and want. Their language skills are rudimentary. They have strong feelings. When their passionate needs are thwarted by us or a peer, they experience intense anger and don't yet know what to do with it. When they lash out, they are doing what they need and want to do at this point in their development. They are not sorry and shouldn't be asked to tell someone that they are.

So, what can you do instead when you want children to transition from using their bodies to using their words? You can choose *your* words wisely. You can describe and define and repeat and understand.

So, what can you do instead when you want children to transition from using their bodies to using their words? You can choose *your* words wisely. You can describe and define and repeat and understand. You can say, "You wanted the horse that Mae-Lin had. When you grabbed it from her, it hit her in the eye. She's crying because it hurt. Let's get some ice to help her eye feel better."

Here's another example. This time you are helping the children develop the concept of personal space. When one toddler pushes another, you might say, "Alexei, Madison is showing me she doesn't want a hug right now. Madison, tell Alexei you want to be alone." Or "Alexei, I think Madison doesn't like you sitting so close. If you sit here, she will have more space." The typical response, "We don't push our friends," doesn't give either child any idea what the problem is or what might be done about it. Indeed, it makes normal social interactions more confusing than they already are to children who are just learning how to be with one another in groups.

It is true that, in recent years, teachers report more and more behavioral challenges with children. In many situations, teachers are unable to alter children's out-of-control behaviors. There are times when a child needs a one-on-one aide and times when a change of program is the only choice. But in the day-to-day world of teaching, your choice of words, tone of voice, and delivery really can make a difference. Many elements are involved in effectively using language to intervene in behavioral situations. Here are some basic guidelines:

- Match your tone of voice and facial expression to the situation.

- If you mean no, say "No!" or "Stop!"

- Avoid vague and wishy-washy requests when you need an immediate response.

- Tell the child what she can do instead of the unacceptable behavior.

- When the inappropriate behavior has stopped, soften your facial expression and support the child in moving to successful alternatives.

Discussion Questions

1. What do you think Lilian Katz means by the statement that adults must accept the authority that is theirs due to knowledge, experience, and wisdom? Can you give some examples from your own experience? When do you find this easy or difficult?

2. What is Gwen Morgan suggesting by differentiating between complicated and complex? Make a list of what is complicated and what is complex in your own work with children and families.

3. Lisa Delpit suggests that white middle-class women feel uncomfortable dealing with class and cultural differences. Do you agree with her? Why or why not? Cite some examples from your work with children and families. Is there a more global way to respond to these dilemmas?

4. Do Dewey and Katz make you or members of your team uncomfortable by challenging you to use the authority that is yours due to age, experience, education, and a need to maintain order now and again when children reject your authority?

5. What words can teachers use to discuss the need for different approaches to behavior in groups as opposed to ideas that work just fine at home with one or two children?

CHAPTER FOUR

Developing Skills and Concepts

IF WE WISH TO GIVE THE CHILDREN in our care every learning advantage possible, we need to become comfortable with fostering a variety of approaches to learning. This might involve broadening our view of how children learn. It also means we need to be lifelong learners ourselves.

Just as chapter 3 suggested the extent to which the media and public press have focused on children's behavior and the "preschool-to-prison pipeline," there has been a steady stream of both popular press and academic articles for the past two decades regarding responses taken to the appropriate approach to entry-level education for our youngest students. The National Association for the Education of Young Children (NAEYC) has worked hard for more than thirty years to provide and update frequent regional presentations on the newest findings in the connections between child growth and development and developmentally appropriate curriculum. Resources are available through NAEYC at very moderate costs to keep teachers of young children up to date on the most current research on child growth and development and the implications of that research for our day-to-day work with young children. The challenge, of course, is that the public demands (for example, by school boards, letters to editors, and the media) for educating the young in our country are continually changing. Often this press is not research based and offers mixed messages about what children truly need. Teachers often feel pressured, confused, ambiguous, guilty, and angry in relation to all of those conflicting demands. Frequently they feel that children and families are getting lost in the process and cycles of change. They also feel confused themselves as to which demands to fulfill: Should they do what they know children need? What families request? What districts determine? What the latest research (which they have no time to read) suggests is best for children? Should they nurture emergent curriculum? Should they teach phonics out of context? What is a teacher to do?

> While some children seem to acquire a range of skills without systematic instruction, most children benefit from individualized instruction and assistance with building specific skills.

While some children seem to acquire a range of skills without systematic instruction, most children benefit from individualized instruction and assistance with building specific skills. Katz and Chard (1989) suggest that many teachers of young children have taken a hands-off approach to skill building because they confuse *systematic instruction* (teaching individual children a progression of skills that contribute to greater proficiency) with *direct instruction* (teaching the same skills at the same time in the same way to a whole class).

Wanting to provide developmentally appropriate environments, teachers of young children shy away from direct instruction, or sitting down a large group of children for instructions at the same time. This is probably a wise decision, in most instances, in terms of meeting the learning needs of very young children or even primary school children.

Using much more casual language, it's training ourselves not to make the quick decision to jump on a bandwagon, as the expression goes. The phrase *jump on the bandwagon* often means *acting before sufficient thought*. Dictionaries describe the idiom as "following something popular." Though most readers will not remember the '60s and '70s phenomenon of the open classroom, it provides the perfect example of jumping on a bandwagon. The notion of opening classrooms for space and interest areas came across the ocean from England in the 1960s. It was well grounded in what we knew and know about children and their development in the early years. It often included ungraded (chronologically) learning and allowed children to do kindergarten-level phonics while doing second-grade math and science if their interests and abilities allowed. But the implementation of this sensible idea (in many instances) was dismal. All over the country, communities, wanting to do well by their children, started ripping down walls and "opening up" their spaces for children to learn in a developmentally appropriate way.

What was missing was the fact that teachers, used to organizing their own classrooms, were often not trained to collaborate or share with their colleagues. It also neglected the very important consideration of introverts, shy and quiet students whose learning style is very solitary. Professionals, families, and children arrived in September to sparklingly revised classrooms—open and free but that met the needs of probably 60 percent of the children, and possibly only 25 percent of the faculty (in the absence of further quality training and orientation to this new way of meeting the children's needs). Teachers, at that point in time, were used to being the voice of the classroom. They were used to imparting what they knew of letters and sounds and numbers, and they usually delivered these lessons to the entire group of children. But now children were to move at their own pace—nothing teachers in the 1960s had been trained to facilitate.

This rapid change without thoughtful preparation of teachers, families, and children is truly a response that has caused us many challenges in our work over the decades. Another example of this is suggesting that the initiative to stop teaching the alphabet out of context to the whole group using direct instruction should be interpreted as the need to remove all alphabet posters from kindergarten and preschool classrooms. We need to make slower decisions. We need to read, think deeply, ponder, reflect, and *then* make our policies. The poet Alexander Pope gave us this sound advice in 1711 in his famous poem, "An Essay on Criticism": "A little learning is a dang'rous thing; / Drink deep." In other words, a quick taste, sip, experience, or read of anything is not adequate to form the foundation of important decisions or policy.

Teachers often fail to give children individual instruction in the basic skills they need to get through the day. Sometimes this is still leftover "conventional wisdom" from the days when we never wanted children to be unhappy, to struggle, or to really stretch to accomplish a goal. We can do a better job with this. We need to make the distinction between individually helping a child improve her competence at using scissors or eating with a fork or writing her name—all skills that are immediately related to the context of her daily life at preschool—and giving group instruction, for instance on the names and appearance of shapes. If children are building a fort in their play yard and the piece of wood they need is rectangular and not square, we have an outstanding opportunity to teach shapes, why they are important, how using the wrong one might have real consequences, and so on. But teaching those same shapes out of context, in a group, with flash cards, recitation, or singing names and shapes is instruction lost on very young children. Children need to learn in a meaningful context that makes sense to them from their day-to-day experiences.

As teachers, we need to remember that the day-to-day experiences of young children in the twenty-first century are, in many ways, very, very different from childhood experiences in the twentieth century— or even ten years ago! In 1899, John Dewey tried to educate us on this necessary and ongoing change. He did much talking with parents about the raising and educating of young children. Parents were concerned that some of the responsibility and character building they had experienced seemed to be disappearing. Dewey cared deeply about social responsibility. He reminded the communities, however, that "it was the social conditions that had changed, and only an equally radical change in education would work in building character" (Tanner 1997, 77). How very contemporary and relevant to our dilemmas that sounds!

When change occurs in a dramatic way, as it did when the former agrarian nature of our workforce and families transitioned to the Industrial Revolution, parents are scared and confused by the changes. These parents had concerns for themselves and their families. They weren't sure just what to do or how to do it. It is said that Dewey was transformative and critically helpful to these families. Though we are nearly two decades into our new century, it seems we all still struggle with our transition to the technological era. Answers to many of our challenges call for that "equally radical change" to education that Dewey prescribed in his era.

When as many of our teachers and their young students clearly struggle on a daily basis with this confusion over conflicting messages and goals, we cannot hope for the positive outcomes we are all capable of. This is a frightening dilemma for teachers, families, school districts, and, most of all, our vulnerable young children as enthusiastic learners. Here is one of these teachers' stories:

Tina attended a workshop about the importance of early literacy for later school success. She was worried about the children she served in her preschool room who would attend public school kindergarten in the fall. She was very aware that most of her students did not know letters or sounds and that many of their peers would be way ahead of them when they started school. She took some of the ideas from her workshop and developed a "word wall." She made a conscious effort to put the alphabet letters all over her room.

She had always worked with children to help them get to know the letter that begins their name, but now she expanded her morning group time to help children learn the initial letters of other people's names and other words that begin with that sound. She added the new words to the word wall. She dramatically sounded out words, stressing initial consonant sounds. She was certain that her four-year-olds were now getting a better preparation for kindergarten. The day I visited her, however, it was her three-year-olds she asked about.

Tina had always had the policy that group time was mandatory for all of the children. We had discussed it many times. I've always thought it too much of a challenge to find an appropriate group time to meet the needs of very young threes, very old fours, and everyone in between. So Tina and I had often discussed a variety of approaches to this topic. This particular day she was feeling discouraged that her threes were suddenly acting out and making group time difficult for everyone. As we talked, it became clear that the behavior issues had begun about the same time she initiated her expanded early literacy work at group time. We talked about the need for fours to work harder on these skills. I also suggested that initial consonant sounds don't thrill three-year-olds too much and maybe there was a connection here.

Tina and I listed the factors we both considered to be part of the dilemma: Tina thought she was providing her fours with necessary systematic instruction but was instead giving a mixed-age group direct instruction in what was a poor developmental match for her young threes. Here is what we concluded the situation involved:

- Although the children are naturally interested in the letters of their own names, the word wall concept and initial consonant work took literacy out of a meaningful context for fours and was completely inappropriate for threes.

- Lack of interest in what was going on made the three-year-olds find other ways to amuse and interest themselves!

- Tina's enthusiasm for early literacy activities needed to be more individualized and matched to the children whose skill level was ready to take that leap.

- Tina could find ways to provide letter recognition or initial sound work in ways that were more developmentally appropriate and also in a more meaningful context.

It was a leap for Tina to decide that her work with her four-year-olds needed to be done at a different time from large group time. In the end, she worked on finding short, wonderfully illustrated alphabet books to share during group instead. She found some new alphabet songs and limited those two activities to the whole group. Next she worked on developing a more sophisticated writing area that was an immediate draw to the children who were both ready and interested in doing serious writing. Little by little, as Tina was able to share the joy of her older students who started writing and reading their own books, she was able to spend her group time in a way that was more suitable for *all* of the children.

Robin had a different approach to working with her four-year-olds. She carefully observed her children during free-play times and then used those notes to guide her planning for the following week. Much of her curriculum was emergent. The emergent interests of children often resulted in wonderful and rich project work. For example, Chris, the assistant teacher, was building a new house. The children went to the construction site to watch. Tools, hard hats, and hammering were soon filling the preschool room. As the children read books about building, took photographs of different kinds of buildings, and brought in pictures of their own homes, the interest heightened. The children started paying more attention to their own school building.

Robin was quick to catch the spirit of their inquiry and was surprised to realize how little they had explored this environment where they gathered every day. She carefully orchestrated an in-depth study that touched on math, literacy, science, and creative arts. The children graphed the different materials in their building. They did crayon rubbings of bricks, boards, and cinder blocks. They mapped the plumbing through their building and watched a plumber replace the wax seal of a toilet in their bathroom. They designed "blueprints" and built structures. They wrote books about their study. Robin had never done a great deal in her woodworking area. Suddenly she found herself taking very seriously the need for direct instruction to the children regarding use of tools, safety goggles, and directions for building bookcases! Notice the extent to which the children's interests guided Robin's instructions and curriculum. The learning throughout this project was deepened because of the meaningful context in which it unfolded and the teacher's intentional and rich response to it.

Respond to Classroom Conversations

When you ask most teachers or parents what the role of a preschool teacher is, the majority will answer that it is to help children get along with other children and to learn the things they need to know before going to school. If asked for clarification, the same groups would say, "You know—how to share, get along, follow directions, and know their colors, shapes, and the alphabet."

As a supervisor of student teachers for many years, I have repeatedly heard students complain that I always managed to observe their program during transitions or mealtimes rather than their group time. Many teachers who are new to the field believe that the real learning goes on when they are front and center with a book or flannel board activity to share with the children. Too often curriculum is evaluated as successful in terms of whether the children enjoyed the activity or sat quietly and attended during the teacher's presentation. However, every day we have opportunities to deepen and extend children's learning and understanding of their world. And too often (because of time, numbers of children in a class, lack of appropriate training, and so on) we don't acknowledge or act on these opportunities. It is an understandable piece of decision making on curriculum content in a community to want expectations to be up to date and forward thinking. Yet some of the fundamental ways that young children have always learned—ways that have been documented and reproduced decade after decade in reputable research studies—are violated on a regular basis in our preschools and primary grades.

In her 2016 book *The Importance of Being Little,* early childhood educator Erika Christakis writes that "preschools worried about not meeting expectations—typically the lower-performing programs and those serving disadvantaged students—embrace . . . comprehensive curriculum packages in the vain hope that they've landed on the magic bullet that will cover the standards and lift achievement scores without any guesswork" (101). As pointed out in chapter 3, however, the situations where teachers are just not quite sure what they should be doing with today's little ones are far more pervasive in all schools than most of us want to acknowledge. Well-funded, upper-middle-class private schools suffer ambivalence just as much as inner-city Head Start programs. This is the result of so many things that, as mentioned in chapter 3, most of us don't even know where to begin. If teachers have not had solid academic training in prereading skills, they are more likely to offer benign activities that children enjoy but are not challenged by. Misunderstanding of developmentally appropriate practices created situations twenty years ago that caused preschools to prevent teachers from hanging alphabet posters in their kindergarten classrooms. This was as absurd as some of today's push-down curriculum that expects children to be reading when they enter first grade.

R. F. Dearden (1984) outlined four criteria for curriculum relevance that can be used to evaluate the kinds of learning opportunities we share with children:

1. Immediate applicability of the topic to children's daily lives

2. Contribution to a balanced school curriculum

3. Value in preparing children for later life

4. Advantage of learning about this in school as opposed to another setting

Katz and Chard (1989) expand on these ideas by suggesting that children's learning must relate to the demands society will make on them. I don't want to discourage teachers from engaging in dinosaur projects or backward clothes days. Fun is important for all of us. It reduces stress and nurtures awareness in children that playfulness is essential to a well-lived life. However, to consider these projects to be well-planned learning while disregarding the responsibility of clarifying misinformation about prisons, weapons, poverty, or skin color is to miss an important piece of our goal as teachers: to assist children to better understand and function in the world we live in. Current social events in our country and around the world make this clear. When we are planning fun activities, we need to be aware that our goals are relaxation, modeling how to balance work and play, and enjoyment. Learning cannot always be fun. Sometimes it's just plain hard work. Gently, we need to introduce this idea to children. We can't underestimate the value of teaching the lesson "if at first you don't succeed, try, try again." It's important to share early on with children that mistakes are a fantastic way to learn many things about what works and what doesn't, how exciting a change of direction can sometimes be and so on. Introducing early on the idea that all of us are much better at some things than we are at others is beneficial. A good example of how to do this (regardless of the age of the child) is to be honest. If Jenny is crying because, once again, she has come in last in a race across the school yard and shouts angrily that no matter how hard she tries she's always last, you can remind her that you had to tell the art teacher that five of Jenny's drawings and paintings were too many for the front bulletin board! "You may never be really good at running, Jenny, but you are a strong reader and great at painting." We are all good at different things. There will be things in life that we just don't do as well as others, so we ask for help from those people. Frequently children of all ages are both very surprised and very pleased to get this feedback from a teacher.

Often teachers are reluctant to address difficult issues with children. It's easy to forget that children will make meaning out of what they experience, with our help or without it. Isn't it better to help them if we can? Here's an example of an issue that surfaced in a Head Start classroom I observed in which the teacher was leading a seemingly innocuous group time about community helpers. The teacher told the children that Officer Friendly would be visiting to share with the children the many ways that their community police helped people in trouble. Joshua leaned over to Carlos and said, "My dad says they are all f****** pigs." The teacher told Josh that the *F*-word "is not a word we use here." She did not address the meaning behind what he said, where this idea might have come from, or the effects of his words on other children in the circle. I continued to observe and heard children talk about "cops" in dramatic play. I saw an "arrest" as well done as any on the evening news coverage of violence in many communities. I heard one child say, "They aren't friendly. They take you to jail." A less sophisticated member of the group said, "What's jail?" A peer quickly chimed in, "It's where the bad guys go!"

Two of the children in this class of seventeen had incarcerated parents. It is a scary thing to address hard and sensitive issues with children, or even with one another. But when we work with young children, we have a responsibility to do so. The fact that many people go to jail is an important thing for children to know, whether there are children whose parents are incarcerated or not. Teaching that we *all* make mistakes and can learn from them is an essential life skill. Teaching children that people are good but sometimes do bad things is also a humane lesson to learn early. When the children had gone, the teacher and I sat down and talked about the day. I asked what she was thinking when she heard the passionate conversations going on in dramatic play. She said she was sad because she knew some of the children had parents in jail. She said they must have felt bad when other children said, "That's where the bad people go." "Could you have done anything to help?" I asked. "I didn't want to get in the middle of it," she said honestly.

I didn't blame her for being hesitant. At the same time, with so much at stake in the lives of young children, teachers can't afford to be afraid of opening a can of worms. It is true that we need to choose words very, very carefully. But it is possible to address children's burning concerns in a way that makes room for all the children's experiences. As we face the dramatic tensions between the wrongs of police brutality and the need to support those who try to keep us safe, children need adults to care and sometimes comment. But discretion and balance are also critical. Teachers can begin by asking questions like "Why do you think so?" or "What do you know about that?" They can acknowledge children's strong feelings with phrases like "Sounds like you really miss your dad," or "Sounds like your dad was really angry at the police." Ultimately, teachers can also frame the different views of the situation for all the children in the room by giving information, saying something like, "All people make mistakes. Sometimes we can learn from them. We need to try to make it right when we do something wrong. When people are in jail, they are trying to make it right for the mistakes they have made." This explanation benefits all of the children in the class. But for the children whose family members are incarcerated, it is essential.

> Teachers can't afford to be afraid of opening a can of worms. It is true that we need to choose words very, very carefully. But it is possible to address children's burning concerns in a way that makes room for all the children's experiences.

Here's another example of a time when seemingly innocuous curriculum strayed into deeper waters and a teacher took on the challenge of addressing difficult issues with children. Stacey was planning curriculum around new babies and being an older sibling, since both Kai and Aisha were expecting new babies at their houses. The work began with lots of new babies to "wash" in the water table and an array of wonderful children's books about new babies. The children had helped their teacher plan a party for Kai and Aisha. The school got them "I'm the Big Brother/Sister" T-shirts, and the children brought in inexpensive gifts for the new babies at Kai's and Aisha's houses.

The light nature of this curriculum changed when three of the girls got into an in-depth discussion of how the whole "baby thing" actually happened. Stacey observed Becky and Aisha playing "pregnant." Baby dolls under their shirts were to be delivered by Dinah, the doctor. Becky insisted that babies get taken out of your belly. With exasperation, Aisha informed her that she had her facts all wrong. "Babies come out of your vagina," she insisted loudly. "And nobody takes them out—they come when they're ready!"

Stacey was a little nervous but proceeded to talk with parents about the children's interest in where babies come from. Jon's mom told the group of children about her cesarean section, pleasing Becky, who was proved correct—some babies do get taken out of people's bellies! The curriculum took a leap from celebration to information, and before the year was over, all of the children knew a great deal more about real human life cycles. Families, however, were aware and approved the curriculum with the teachers before they went ahead with the children's emerging interests. For the many sensitive issues discussed in chapter 6, this is not a typical preschool curriculum unit, and consensus with everyone involved would be essential.

Teach Basic Skills

Teachers help children learn with the environments they create, the experiences they provide, the conversations they engage in, the questions they ask, and the encouragement they give children to think for themselves. Teachers also support children's learning by teaching them important concepts and assisting them in developing essential skills. Here are some essential skills young children are learning:

- self-help skills (buttoning, zipping, tying)
- using glue and scissors
- using eating utensils
- pumping a swing
- pedaling a tricycle
- washing hands and brushing teeth
- taking turns
- expressing their own wants and needs
- understanding others' wants and needs
- negotiating conflict
- solving problems

Children will not develop these skills without systematic instruction from parents and teachers. We need to provide children with facts and tools and with the knowledge of how to use these facts and tools to discover more about the world around them. This is very different from giving an entire class, ready or not, direct instruction on how to write a poem, hold a pencil, or zip a zipper.

Throughout the day, children present teachers with many, many opportunities to teach, to make meaning, and, yes, to correct their unclear or incorrect understanding of real-world objects and ideas. Often teachers forget that free play is an excellent time to make the most of individualizing learning for young children.

Psychologist Kathleen McCartney (1984) provides us with evidence that children truly need intentional efforts on the part of teachers to help them develop language skills and ideas. Children simply chatting with each other as they play do not provide each other with adequate stimulation or enough meaning to polish their intellectual skills. McCartney's study randomly selected children from seven child care centers (of varying quality) where verbal interactions were observed and recorded. Children were later evaluated on several language and cognitive scales. Her results indicated that the quality of the child care environment and the amount of verbal interaction between children and adults were clear predictors of how children scored on cognitive and language measures. The study measured not only the amount but also the kind of verbal interaction. High-scoring children had teachers who used fewer controlling and more information-giving conversations with children.

For the past twenty years, one of the most clichéd phrases repeatedly discussed in education has been the "30 million–word gap." A recent article (Sparks 2015, 1) had this to say of the study: "

> The "30 million–word" gap is arguably the most famous but least significant part of a landmark study, *Meaningful Differences in the Everyday Experiences of Young Children*, by the late University of Kansas child psychologists Betty Hart and Todd R. Risley. As the work turns 20 this year, new research and more advanced measuring techniques have cast new light on long-overshadowed, and more nuanced, findings about exactly how adult interactions with infants and young children shape their early language development." But for many of us, it now represents one of those "jump on the bandwagon" situations.

Put simply, "the gap" refers to the difference between the number of words children of an upper-middle-income family have accumulated in their early years compared to the number (and kind) of words children in economically limited households have acquired by the same chronological age. Not surprisingly, upper-income families tend to focus on "learning" words. Often families living under constant stress tend to use more directive words: "stop," "no," "now," or "I mean it!" As a person who has lived at both ends of this spectrum, I understand that (Bronfenbrenner's context is critical here) the gap is not as simple as how many words does which child have at what age!

We also know that child-to-child conversation is equally as important for young children as teacher-to or teacher-with child conversations. Vygotsky reminded us that social interaction with multiage humans is critical to children's development. Vygotsky termed children's "sense making" verbalizations *private speech*. The practice is at its height between ages four and six years of age. Eventually it becomes quiet muttering and then internalized speech or thought (Anthony 2017). As I read the "quiet muttering," I realized not all of us outgrow this entirely. I'm sure I'm not the only one on the planet who has responded to a colleague or friend, "Oh . . . nothing! I was just talking to myself." Think about it. This usually happens when we are formalizing a plan, idea, or approach but haven't quite got it. For children, this is a stage of development, one that lasts a fairly long time. For us, it is a quick return to something that worked! (For more on Vygotsky, my *Theories of Childhood*, second edition, is included in the resources section.)

Most of us do not have an extensive background in the very process of language development or how teachers can and must nurture it in our work with children. Again, I refer readers to NAEYC publications for excellent resources that provide basic information or reminders, if that's what you need. As discussed thoroughly in the previous chapter, there are multiple reasons that leave many of us unprepared to do the work we are doing well. One of those reasons was brought up in the previously cited article about quality of conversations (Sparks 2015). W. Steve Barnett, director of the National Institute for Early Education Research at Rutgers University, said of the word-gap phenomenon and its attending effect on push down curricula, "This is the challenge of translating science to policy, and when one study captures the imagination of the public, and policy is made based on one study. [A study] has to be viewed in the context of the much larger body of knowledge about language and family and experience" (Sparks 2015, 11).

> Teaching facts supports children's learning. Teaching thinking and reasoning supports children's learning. Their use and purposes are different, but both are essential in nurturing language and intellectual development.

Teachers sometimes hesitate to provide information to children because they have been cautioned against dominating the day with teacher talk. While it is true that we want to listen to children and encourage their language, it is also true that we need to model language and teach concepts as children question possibilities during their play. Teaching facts supports children's learning. Teaching thinking and reasoning supports children's learning. Their use and purposes are different, but both are essential in nurturing language and intellectual development.

Facts are helpful to children. Expanding a child's vocabulary of simple concept words (*hard, soft, wet, dry, hot, cold,* and so forth) helps the child make accurate descriptions or repeat information correctly. By learning facts, children become more competent at describing, listening, repeating, recalling, and following directions.

The higher-level skills required for divergent thinking (thinking that leads to many options and possibilities) and mental reasoning call on children's advanced cognitive development as well as on teachers' skills at questioning and nurturing creative solutions. Another important role of the teacher is to extend and correct information that surfaces as children test ideas and even stereotypes during their dramatic play.

So, what can teachers do about all of this? The first step is to respond to children's questions and statements in the classroom and to engage children in conversations during free-play times. Here are some examples of children's statements I have heard in the last year during free play. All of these offered learning opportunities that teachers ignored—and can't afford to ignore!

- "Dogs can't swim—just fish!"
- "Girls are the nurses."
- "You can't put the little one under the big one—it won't work."
- "Only girls wear the ballet shoes. Boys don't dance."
- "If you mix the red and blue paint, you just get black."
- "If it's bigger, it makes the scale go down."

All of these statements could use some careful questioning and clarification from the teacher or experimentation and validation by the children! It is a teacher's responsibility to make meaning for children as well as to respect each child's family and values. This calls for thoughtful responses. We need to listen and think before we speak, but we must speak. If children have been arguing in dramatic play that Isha can't be the doctor because she is a girl, we need to listen to what has been said. Did Travis say his dad said girls are the nurses and boys are the doctors? The best approach may be a cautious one. For example, an attentive teacher might offer different information by saying something like "That's interesting, Travis. You know, my sister had a baby last week, and the doctor was a woman."

It is helpful to children when teachers interject language that helps them think things through for themselves. Here are some examples:

- What makes you think that?

- Could you try it and see what happens?

- Can you think of another way to do it?

- What do you know about this?

- What did you try?

- Why do you think that is so?

- Has anyone ever seen a (boy dancer, woman doctor, dog swimming)?

- Sometimes that's true, but I wonder what would happen if . . .

- Has anyone taken their dog to the beach? What happened?

Another way of correcting uninformed information we hear from children is to conduct an experiment. Test out the children's statements, and see if they are true or not. This is the basic scientific inquiry process. For example, I have often heard preschoolers say you can't grow vegetables inside because plants need dirt, water, and sun. How about an experiment to find out if you have to plant seeds outside in order for them to grow? Children are fascinated as they realize that the sun coming through the window works just like the sun outside, that if you don't water your plant it really will die, and that sometimes you do everything you were supposed to and the plant still dies. The lessons are many! The lessons for teachers are many as well.

Let's go back to the preschool teacher reading *Green Eggs and Ham* at story time. Here's the story again: "I'll begin the story when everyone is sitting nicely!" the teacher said. The children continued to wiggle and squirm. The teacher became increasingly agitated. Finally, her assistant said, "C'mon, kids, we need to crisscross applesauce here." The teacher began reading *Green Eggs and Ham*. As usual, the children had comments right off the bat. "There aren't really no green eggs." "Are too, like you get in your Easter basket." "Those aren't real eggs." "Are too." (Louder.) "No!" (Louder still.) Here the teacher interrupted the discussion, saying, "Inside voices." The children ignored her, and her own inside voice got louder. "Inside voices!" she asserted loudly. "We need to get back to our story!" The children settled down again, but several of them were clearly still thinking about the question of green eggs and whether they really exist! At the end of the story, the teacher asked, "What happened?" The children said in unison, "He liked the green eggs and ham." The teacher beamed and said, "So, you see, we should always have a no-thank-you bite, because we have to try things. We can't say we don't like something if we never tried it."

In chapter 2, we talked about the vague directions the teacher gave the children when she wanted specific behaviors from them. But there is something else going on here too. The teacher focused on the children's behaviors using phrases like "inside voices," "crisscross applesauce," and "no-thank-you bites" instead of following up on the learning and experimental possibilities that had presented themselves. What might have happened if she had returned to the subject of real eggs and whether they are green? A difference of opinion is such a wonderful opportunity for learning. It's always tempting to end the conflict instead of clarifying the different ideas—what could this teacher have done instead?

- Children could have cracked open many eggs to see if any were green.
- The teacher could offer to bring in the kind of candy eggs one child had mentioned.
- Children could have dyed white eggs green.
- The teacher could have engaged the children in more in-depth conversation about eggs (green or otherwise) to let them

experiment with words, ideas, concepts, and learning from each other.

She might have asked questions like these:

- What makes you so sure there are no green eggs?
- Why do you think Jenny knows there are green eggs?
- How and why do things change color?

Knowing just when and how to respond to children's questions and challenges in the face of the teacher's own agenda is always a challenge. Here's a story that shows a teacher switching gears with finesse when a simple group time on "our families" led to discussions of hurt, anger, and divorce. Glenda had read a story about families that was warm and pleasant but not sugary. She followed up with talk about loving the people in our families. Four-year-old Nadim didn't want to hear it. "Not me!" he shouted. Glenda sweetly responded that sometimes we get mad at the people in our families, but we always love them. "Not me!" Nadim shouted more loudly and passionately. "It sounds like you are really mad at someone in your family this morning," Glenda said gently. The floodgates were opened, and Nadim cried that his dad yelled and left and now his mom was getting a divorce. "I hate them," he said. Glenda was a bit relieved when Samantha said, "My dad left, and I don't hate him. He makes us spaghetti at his new apartment." "Families make us feel lots of things," Glenda said. She quickly reached for a book on feelings and read it with the children. When they were finished, she offered choices to the children, including staying with her to draw or write stories about families and feelings. Many children moved on, but many stayed right there, talking about their own feelings when parents were angry or when children felt scared and sad. What is important about Glenda's story is her recognition of Nadim's immediate need. She also tactfully allowed children not needing to talk or interested in talking the opportunity to go elsewhere, but she was able to set aside her plans to do the real, important work of early educators: helping children understand their world and all the wonderful and difficult things that includes!

Ask Questions

One of the best ways that teachers can stimulate children's thinking and learning is by asking good questions. Making statements instead of asking questions can sometimes put an end to a discussion that offers great possibilities for children to learn from each other or from their own misinformation. As teachers, our repertoire of questions is always in need of expansion and practice.

The dictionary defines *question* as "an expression of inquiry that invites or calls for a reply; a subject open to controversy; an unsettled issue." When I think of questions frequently asked of young children in preschool, it's hard to find the controversy, the unsettled issue. Below are questions I hear frequently:

- What shape is this?

- What letter is this?

- Who is line leader today?

- Whose turn is it?

- Do you like pancakes?

- What is your favorite color?

- Did you hear me?

It is sad but somewhat true that many teachers still think part of teaching is getting children to give us the "right" answer. It is also true that many teachers are required to use methods and record responses in a way that is not appropriate to teaching very young children. They struggle to keep on balance between district demands, children's developmental as well as chronological ages, parental expectations, and often extremely wide ranges of abilities that are not necessarily met by the materials they must implement and require of children regardless of the match between the task and the child. Many of the early educators I listen to describe their daily ethical struggles with how well they are doing by the children in their care.

One of the encouraging emerging areas of study is the exploration of resilience. Researchers are beginning to look at some of the strengths children develop when they are forced to face adversity as children. None of us wants to welcome or affirm stressful childhoods for any children. But given that throughout history most children have had to face some kind of adversity on their way to adulthood, looking at the strengths and not just the vulnerabilities that result might help us all do a better job with the children and families we serve. Be sure to check out Megan Hustad's article "Up from Chaos" in the resources section.

We are also conditioned to ask questions to which we already know the answer. Children either sense our insincerity or sometimes are genuinely perplexed, like the boy who, when asked what color his shirt was, replied, "Wow, Teacher, you still don't know your colors!" The purpose of a question is to get information that we don't already know. Remember that basic guideline: never ask a question to which you already know the answer. This applies to supporting children's learning as well as to guiding their behavior. Philosophers through the ages remind us that we learn more by looking for the answer to a question and not finding it than we do from learning the answer itself. If this is true, we certainly want to develop better skills for asking questions requiring a search or much discussion.

I met a teacher who was masterful at creating months of curriculum, begun with a simple question. Here is her story: Judy believes children are never too young to be exposed to fine art. Her room has changing art exhibits of both child and adult art, still lifes, portraits, and fascinating prints of medieval paintings, complete with busy streets where vendors call and dogs bark. I am fascinated by the work she can introduce with a few simple questions. "Why do people paint?" she asked at group time one May morning. Here is what children said:

- "Because their moms don't let them at home!"
- "Because they like the way the colors look."
- "Because they want to remember something like a walk with their papa."
- "Because their car gets wrecked and needs the scratches gone."
- "Because they like the way the paint runs down the page when Cindy puts too much water in!"

- "Because their moms like it on the 'frigerator.'"
- "Because Grandma says the house should be a different color."
- "Because the teacher says it's your turn."

Judy wrote all of these reasons on a large poster board. Then she asked questions about each response:

- Why don't moms let you paint?
- What is it you like about the colors?
- How does the picture help you remember?
- Do they paint the car with a brush? How does it happen?
- How is the paint different when there is too much water?
- Why do moms like pictures on the refrigerator?
- Why does Grandma want the house to look different?
- How is it different to paint when the teacher says it's your turn than when you just decide you want to paint?

I was fascinated at the depth of conversation that followed with Judy's five-year-olds. When Judy does a project, it lasts for a long time. She showed children a huge variety of paintings, one day at a time, recording their thoughts and feelings about each one. Some were scary. Some were interesting. Some were just pretty, others *beautiful*! Each day she would ask "Why?" and "Why?" and "Why?" in response to the children's comments. She had the children offering critique and explaining to peers why the painting made them sad, scared, interested. I was with her the day the children took a field trip to the Currier Gallery of Art. The adults at the museum were amazed that a group of children so young had such a high level of interest, asked so many interesting questions, and offered such sophisticated comments. My intent is not to be simplistic. Much was involved in this long project. But I continue to believe that the course was set that first day when, instead of saying, "Today we are going to talk about painting," Judy began her group time with the question, "Why do people paint?"

How can teachers develop these skills? The quick answer is to ask more *open-ended* questions (those that allow for multiple responses).

Open-ended questions are associated with nurturing *divergent thinking* (producing many options or possibilities, which may result in unusual solutions), while *closed* questions (those requiring one correct answer) are associated with nurturing *convergent thinking* (putting all the pieces together to generate one solution).

Teachers develop convergent thinking skills by asking closed questions like these:

- Whose turn is it?

- Is it a fruit or a vegetable?

- How many legs does it have?

- Is it little or big?

- Where does it live?

Teachers develop divergent thinking skills by asking open-ended questions like these:

- What do you think?

- What would happen if . . . ?

- What else could you do?

- What could you do to fix it?

- How could you help her understand?

Even when teachers want to foster inquiry, they sometimes need simple yes and no answers to questions. For instance, if you are planning a field trip, it might be important to know who has been to the fire station, a car wash, or an ice cream factory and who has not. Clearly, if you are looking for a word that rhymes with *cat*, there are many correct answers, but *ball* is not one of them. There are certainly abundant reasons to ask questions that require a yes or no or right or wrong answer. As teachers, we also want to ensure abundant opportunities for children to think creatively, stretch their imaginations, and test their intuition. Open-ended questions help teachers do this. They also encourage children to talk more, which stretches their vocabulary and helps them get better at expressing themselves in words. That's what preliteracy is all about!

Here are some guidelines to supporting young children's emerging thinking through teacher talk:

- Be sincere and authentic.

- Try to ask questions that nurture divergent thinking.

- Limit questions requiring yes or no answers.

- Increase your comfort level with not knowing the answer; join the children in searching for it.

- If you already know the answer, don't ask the question.

- Practice conversation starters like "What do you know about mice, Sammy?" rather than "Is this a mouse?"

- Start a conversation with "What do you know about this?"

- Welcome brainstorming ideas even with very young children.

- Validate children for suggesting solutions that couldn't possibly work!

- Acknowledge the importance of both content learning and critical thinking.

- Encourage fact finders with questions like "What did you see?" "How do you know?" "Does it have a name?"

- Encourage critical thinkers with questions like "Why do you think it melted?" "Why do you think this happened?" "What would happen if the wind didn't blow?"

- Observe children carefully and regularly to know which emerging skills to assist.

- Give children time to ponder.

Don't jump in too quickly to solve problems or offer accurate information. Wrong solutions offer great learning when active thinking is going on.

Many of these approaches do not answer the questions of either teachers or parents regarding the extent to which experimentation with curricula approaches helps or hinders the education of young children in America. We continue to ask questions about ABCs and

123s, rather than asking questions about what the essential learnings should be to help the next generation manage the challenges of a future we cannot even imagine. Changing the outcomes for our young children is hard to imagine without time to educate and reflect with America's teachers. However, there are resources available.

As pointed out in previous chapters, children and families need certain basic things to effectively become an informed and active part of their communities. The criteria for these skills and competencies and the means to achieving them are specific to the cultural, regional, political, economic, and other factors associated with regions, counties, countries, and the like. But the basic needs have been outlined and documented for generations—regardless of who we are or where we live. As Bronfenbrenner (1979) pointed out nearly half a century ago, most of these things are basic human needs for human caring, curious learning, and a sense of community. Making clear statements about how young children learn most easily is not a newly discovered area of scientific inquiry.

Here's a list of some common learning opportunities for children:

- play
- watching others
- experiences
- experimenting
- doing
- ideas from peers
- imitating peers
- mistakes (an enormous source of learning for all ages)
- adults (conversations, modeling, systematic instruction)
- warm relationships
- listening
  - to music
  - to the sound garbage trucks make

- to the sounds heating systems make
- to the sounds you can make with your mouth, your hands, your whole body

- exposure to quality children's literature

- exposure to quality early learning materials

- exposure to unique materials and recyclables as well as abundant open spaces of time for exploring and creating with these materials

- adults in one's learning environment who possess an understanding of the importance of all of the above to the learning process

The last example should motivate us to look more carefully at the role of teachers in extending children's learning. On the surface, it seems such a simple thing and one to which most of us would respond, "Well, of course!" My observations of teachers and examination of conscience tell me that we are not as good at this as we would like to think.

One of the country's leading experts on children and families, Ellen Galinsky, is the president and cofounder of the Work and Families Institute and longtime professor at Bank Street College of Education. In her book *Mind in the Making* (2010), Galinsky outlines the seven essential skills every child needs to survive and thrive in the world as we currently know it. Those of us who were raised with a focus on reading and counting, may find it challenging to read about and accept these skills as the way to the future for the next generation. But if we return to Dewey (1899), we should recognize the message. We need to change as time and culture move forward. I conclude the chapter with Galinsky's essential skills:

- focus and self-control

- perspective taking

- communicating

- making connections

- critical thinking
- taking on challenges
- self-directed, engaged learning

Discussion Questions

1. What skills and concepts do you hope to develop in the young children in your care? Pick one or two of the most important ones. How might you use teacher talk to help support children's development of these skills or concepts?

2. What do you think are some of the barriers to strong skill development? Is there anything that can be done to change these?

3. What do you think is the difference between "dispositions for learning" and actual skill development? Why are both important? What can you do to nurture both in the children you care for?

4. How do you respond to parental concern that you don't appear to engage in enough direct instruction?

5. What would you say to a parent who questions the need for critical thinking on the part of second graders?

CHAPTER FIVE

Conversations, Discussions, and Stories

RESEARCH TELLS US THAT CHILDREN who spend their time in conversation-rich environments become better speakers, readers, writers, and thinkers than their peers not exposed to abundant quality language experiences. Research also confirms that for years, classrooms have been dominated by teacher talk and that most of that talk takes the form of directives rather than invitations to verbal inquiry or complex discussion. We know that language is the key to all other kinds of content learning. Yet we often deny children the opportunity to question, disagree, conjecture, or play with language in a way that builds their communication skills and vocabulary.

Creating Conversation-Rich Environments

Conversation–rich environments could be described as places where there are meaningful conversations as well as "just talking." I am a big proponent of "just talking," so I don't want to confuse the reader. In chapter 4, we talked about the difference between planned activities that have the sole purpose of fun and those that also offer children skills they will need to get through life. The rationale for fun activities was that we are modeling for children the importance of things like relaxing, dreaming, and letting our minds wander. This is different from a study, say, in which children watch and wait for eggs to hatch, observe the eggs in an incubator, keep records on and make charts and graphs about the eggs, and are responsible for the care and feeding of new baby chicks. Both kinds of curriculum planning are essential to a well-rounded preschool, kindergarten, or primary-grade program.

Meaningful conversation and just talking play similar roles in a conversation-rich environment to those varied curricula-planning strategies for concept development. Both meaningful conversation and just talking are important to a child's language development, and both occur in a conversation-rich environment.

A conversation-rich environment offers a variety of components that allow language development to flourish. Here are three of the most important:

- a large gathering area for group conversations
- a comfortable area for more intimate conversations
- a comfortable space for solitude

GROUP CONVERSATION

Conversation in a group is an important part of any language-learning environment. This is where group singing or dancing occurs. It is where a local farmer talks to children about her work with bees, prior to a field trip to visit her farm. This is where teachers share a group story or poem, or inform children of a new policy or a need for more attention to detail at pickup time. Ideally, it is located at the other end of the room from an interest area for those not interested in optional whole-group stories, singing, or other activities.

INTIMATE CONVERSATION NEEDS

Conversations with fewer people require small sofas, comfortable chairs, or cushions where a few children can share a book or a more intimate conversation out of the way of block building, dress-up, or math materials. This is an area where teachers can read one-on-one or read to a few children books, stories, or poetry that are not a good match for all of the children or even a semilarge group experience. Many children, even throughout elementary school, are not yet comfortable with prolonged or interesting conversation in front of a group of many others. However, friendships can develop over a mutual interest in insects, for example, when there are spaces and materials to nurture and support such learning—even if no one else in the class is into mosquitoes! Those of you who are already thinking your room cannot accommodate all or even most of these special spaces should explore some of the wonderful books on environments available (see the resource section); they offer an array of creative solutions to classroom space. I observed in a classroom where the teacher had taken doors off of a coat closet, hung a lantern over the light fixture, and lined the entire space with comfy cushions and a couple of baskets of great books. On the wall was a framed fine art poster of children reading. It was captivating! Baskets of books that include a good variety of both topics and skill levels are a must for every area in a conversation-rich environment.

SPACES FOR SOLITUDE

One might immediately ask the question, "What does solitude have to do with nurturing language development and rich conversation?" It is an excellent question and one that is pretty easy for us to answer if we pause and reflect a bit. Most of us are "treated" to music while we are on hold for a conference call, while we are grocery shopping, or even when taking a fairly brief ride in an elevator. We stop for a sandwich and get adequate food in an establishment that has six or eight large screens, all on different channels, offering news, sports, and The Shopping Channel. Language development, like most other areas of development, is complex and simultaneously works on many criteria. For children to build a strong foundation in language learning, many components are necessary.

This list includes some of these components:

- teachers who know about language development
- opportunities that nurture ongoing conversation (both formal and informal)

- learning approaches that are effective for introverts as well as extroverts

- a variety of quality children's books as well as less formal books that children might already have a comfort level with (shhh!— grocery store Little Golden Books might be an example), magazines, and sale brochures from the newspaper

- modeling of fine conversation skills

- teachers who continually make the connection for children between thinking and talking

- teachers who continually model the real-life connection between reading, speaking, and living (an example: "Let's look for the directions in the box. They will tell us how to put our new water table together!")

- teachers who respond, "I'll have to think about that for a while," modeling that thinking, speaking, and acting are all group, collaborative, and solitary experiences

Current research on the impact of media on all of us suggests that there are fewer and fewer places where we can hide from the constant barrage of media and noise. While all of the above components are critical, children also require times of solitude to rest and allow their brains the chance to make sense of all this input and form the connections required for language development. Some children require more solitude than others. Adults can choose to make that happen in their lives. We can take a walk in the woods or by the ocean. We can decline social invitations. We can articulate that we need a bit of solitude in order to think. Children are not afforded these optional pleasures. Teachers wanting to foster conversation and language development need to create and explain solitude for children.

In previous chapters, we have discussed the frustration teachers feel when they know the importance of all of the above to the skill building and language development of the next generation, yet appropriate spaces and uninterrupted pockets of time to provide for rich and interesting conversations are not made a priority in schools or get crowded out by competing priorities. It is also easy for us, managing so many demands, to use "the system" as an excuse for not finding creative solutions like the one illustrated above by the teacher who created space for solitude in a coat closet.

Creating such an environment also requires that we, as adults, choose our words with care as we have conversations and discussion with young children. Think for a minute about the times you have heard teachers say, "Listen," or "Be quiet, please," compared with the number of times you've heard teachers say, "What do you think?" or "Tell me all about it!" We are not doing the best we can at encouraging meaningful conversation. The seriousness of this fact today is compounded by the reality that family time for meaningful conversation has also been reduced in recent years because of the pace of life in this country and parental stresses of balancing work and family life. Children in the United States fall way behind their peers in other countries when it comes to either meaningful family time or community time (Span 2010). Common Sense Media recently sponsored a commercial urging parents to make mealtimes device-free times. It features a fabulous little preschool fellow who tries to tell his parents about his day at preschool while they answer with disinterest as they focus on their cell phones. Both parents and teachers need to remember that as device use and technology take more and more of adults' attention, our children need our attention to ongoing quality conversations, storytelling, and reading great books. These conversations, our focused attention, and body language and facial expressions that indicate our interest and delight in sharing this time with them will help them learn to use and love language and its many functions.

Using Words within a Meaningful Context

Though abundant attention has been paid to differences in the number of words children know and understand from birth to age five (Putnam 2015) (Hart and Risley 1995), the meaningful context of words and their use has mostly been ignored in the conversations. Too many studies have posed only problems without suggesting alternatives or solutions. There are things we can do to help families and teachers cope with the stresses of a constant barrage of criticism that declining test scores or language development is the fault of both parents and teachers. Below are a few winning suggestions from veteran teachers:

- In the resource section are many articles and books about our current national language crisis as well as some of its causative factors. Rotate staff responsibility for reducing an important article or chapter to a single page of bullet points. Send out once a week in family pages. Post online so busy families have easy access.

- Have an evening or weekend family meeting with a provocative title such as "How much viewing is too much viewing?" "How can wide-screen TVs in a restaurant affect a two-year-old?" or (my personal favorite) "If your child never shouts, always goes to bed willingly, is compliant with parental concerns about safety, and has never embarrassed you in public, don't bother to attend. You'll be bored!" Then discuss supporting families as a societal challenge.

- Barter with colleagues to be a presenter in their classrooms and they in yours so parents and teachers don't feel they are always listening to the same voice.

- Maintain a file box with articles parents can always help themselves to. It is true that most of us head to Google for information, but when you develop trusting relationships with both colleagues and families—and they are struggling with behavior or communication challenges at home or school—they will be grateful that you have already done some footwork.

- At a recent conference, a participant referenced the numbers of grandparents who are raising children today. The veteran teacher said she had gotten out of the habit of providing paper copies of anything, as all teachers and parents use their phones to access everything. She said her file box of paper copies was used by all of the grandparents, but she was surprised by the number of very young parents who foraged the file box for articles on what to read to or with children, and on explaining the complexity of words used at home (and why they are not shouted in supermarkets!)

Teachers and child care workers want to do the best they possibly can for the children in their care. Professional associations, school districts, and state departments of Health and Human Services (DHHS) need to find ways to offer those who are actually spending their days with our youngest children basic, user-friendly information about meaningful communication and language development. For those wanting to know how to accomplish this support in a low-budget way, here are some ideas:

- Providing basic information on child development and language development is not a huge challenge for well-trained early educators. Have someone who is qualified to do so add this information to the state orientation, Department of Education (DOE), or child care licensing information packet.

- Make the information a part of DOE or DHHS orientation online.

- Provide new employees with the contact people in your state for DOE or ECE professional associations.

- If your state still does in-person orientation, offer NAEYC, Redleaf Press, Teachers College Press, and Gryphon House catalogs in your orientation folder so individuals can select the grade level and information that matches their situation.

- Articulate to staff the need to subscribe to at least one appropriate professional journal—and *read* it monthly. This is an important piece of administrative responsibility.

In response to pressure to close the performance gap between different groups of our young children, we have forgotten the need for individualization. However, as budget struggles continue at both the state and national level, we need to be realistic about the fact that teacher training costs time and money. The general public often has no idea how hard their children's teachers are working or how important it is for parents and nonparents, married couples and single people, Democrats and Republicans to care about this issue. I once saw an advocacy response to the question "Why should my taxes increase for more and better schools? I have no children." Answer: "Your neighbor's two-year-old may one day be doing your heart surgery!"

Expecting early childhood and elementary trained teachers to broadly implement the same curriculum to children of differing abilities and developmental ages, as well as immigrant and refugee children who are new to the country and completely without knowledge of English (or even a strong grasp of their families' languages if they are only in preschool!) is an unrealistic expectation.

Teaching words in isolation without grounding them in a meaningful context, for the sake of increasing numbers of vocabulary words recognizable to children, does not improve learning for any of our children. Each of these special children needs something different in an approach to her or his language development. Their teachers and families need support in finding out what is needed and where it can be accessed. I have observed and tried (but not succeeded) in supporting teachers who are struggling with this challenge. One cannot expect to be successful at increasing language development for very young children, in English, if they are still adjusting to a move of family and change in lifestyle that is life altering. Taking that pressure off of teachers is probably helpful in and of itself.

However, the suggestions provided above for creating conversation-rich environments can be helpful, especially if you have two children from the same linguistic background. If the children can pore over interesting picture books in their own (newly building) language, you are supporting their language development. Making children feel comfortable might seem unrelated, but it isn't. Photos, well matted and welcoming in an entrance hall of families from around the world, say, "Welcome . . . we are trying! We are building a classroom community here."

It might seem obvious that a language-rich environment for young children includes conversation between caregivers and the children. Yet for any number of reasons, most adults are much better at talking *at* children than they are at talking *with* them. This is met with a number of responses from children. One response is to tune us out. Another is to slowly lose the wonder and passion for life that seem to accompany most children into the world. If adults' responses to children's excitement and discovery and their verbal attempts to share those is met with a distracted "Uh-huh," or "That's not what we are discussing, Taylor!" it is no wonder that, over time, the children fall silent. They also respond by building rehearsed, dull, automatic answers to adults whom they perceive as not really interested.

Although the world of adult communication has experienced numerous changes in recent years with the influx of new technology, the needs of children in this area have remained constant. I think of the many essential things that are still relevant, including the following:

- listening to children

- taking time to ponder what they are really trying to say

- asking, "Are we trying to really make the time to figure out what is on their minds?"

- considering whether teachers know how developmentally appropriate it is for children, in the midst of group conversation, to jump from a house that is blue to a car that is blue to a car going too fast

Jim Greenman (1993, 33) described this perfectly in his classic article "Just Wondering: Building Wonder into the Environment." He tells us of his observation of unsought instruction as a mother and her four-year-old share a trip to the zoo:

"Look, Johnny, flamingos!" the mother exclaimed. "What are they?"
"Birds," said Johnny.
"What color are they?"
"Pink," said Johnny.
"How many are there?"
"Three," said Johnny.

Two giraffes lumbered into view. Before Johnny's determined mom could open her mouth, Johnny called out: "Giraffes, yellow, two." Johnny had overdosed on teachable moments. Wonder comes from a child's search and discovery, not from our dutiful prodding.

Note, too, that Johnny's mother had disregarded one of the prime guidelines for conversations with young children: never ask a question you know the answer to. Johnny's mom doubtless knew what kinds of animals she was looking at, what color they were, and how many there were.

While most parents do not have the opportunity to attend ECE classes where they would learn not to ask questions they already know the answer to, ECE teachers do have this training and yet too often we do the same thing! We continue to do this on a regular basis with the children in our care, even though mentors like Jim Greenman have taught us to do differently. We are less forgivable for our mistakes in this area than parents, who get a few prenatal classes and then are on their own! It seems like a simple mistake for parents to make because parents receive so little help with this enormous job we continue to (mostly) joyfully take on.

But as ECE teachers, we should know better. We should be doing a better job at helping each other realize what the most frequent mistakes we make are and how we can help each other and future generations of ECE teachers avoid these mistakes. As we revisit these issues almost two decades into the twenty-first century, we have sociological issues to ponder that were barely on the radar screen when *Use Your Words* was first published. Just as the world of research is often slow to reach those who need the latest findings, so too is the pace at which teacher education can keep up with the changing times.

The wonder children bring to our classrooms can easily be snuffed out when we focus solely on our plan for children's learning rather than carefully listening to the children and following their conversational lead. This can be a real challenge, since we know young children speak from a pretty egocentric place: one child's response to a teacher's question about jungle animals gives birth to another child's discussion of his uncle's car. This is what will sometimes happen in a conversation with four-year-olds—or even seven-year-olds!

Here's a conversation I observed in a preschool classroom. The teacher, talking about wild animals, asked the children if they knew names of any wild animals.

Juan immediately said, "Tiger."

This triggered some unsolicited conversation from Todd, who said, "My uncle's car is called Tiger. It's yellow, goes really, really fast, and my auntie says my uncle loves that car more than her!"

The teacher responded quickly, and typically, "We are talking about animals today, Todd, not cars." Sometimes teachers must do a particular lesson and keep it moving because of other demands on the schedules. Sometimes we could easily follow through on a child's train of thought and leave our agenda for later, but acknowledging children's contributions, even if briefly, is respectful and important.

For the rest of the jungle discussion, Todd was tuned out. He fidgeted, looked around, and didn't listen. He probably had hurt feelings as well as questions about what he had said to elicit such an uninterested and abrupt response. I wondered what would have happened had she said simply, "Why do you think he calls the car Tiger, Todd?" I didn't wonder about Todd's involvement with the rest of her circle time as much as what would have happened to this circle time discussion. Perhaps someone would have shouted, "Tigers are yellow," or "Tigers have stripes—does his car have stripes?" I can picture someone else saying, "Maybe because they both go really fast." Children would have conversed, questioned, come to conclusions. The teacher could have made connections and congratulated the children on their work. Todd would feel that he made a contribution. Instead, he felt he'd done the wrong thing and wasn't even sure why.

The wonder children bring to our classrooms can be snuffed out when we focus solely on our plan for children's learning rather than carefully listening to the children and following their conversational lead.

Here's another example. A teacher took her children to the woods to gather autumn leaves. When the children found a fallen tree covered with ants, they were amazed. Here are some of their comments:

- "Wow—there must be a million!"
- "Are they born in the tree?"
- "No! Man, they all climbed up there when it fell over!"
- "How do you know?"
- "Is he right, Teacher?"

Unfortunately, the teacher didn't address how the ants got there or where the children's guesses came from. "Come along, class," she said. "We are here to find leaves!" I have observed this response over and over and know I often did this too as a kindergarten teacher, even after I had been given excellent instruction in why it didn't support the children's own emerging thoughts and directions. Teachers know what happens here. The principal wants autumn leaves spatter painting for parents' night, progress reports are due Friday, and I took a professional day to go on a field trip for my son's school . . . etc., etc., etc. Sometimes when I look back and reflect, I wonder why I didn't set out orange, yellow, and red paint, matte the children's work, do a bulletin board with some branches of leaves stapled up there too, and perfect calligraphy saying, "Welcome, Parents!" In most cases, our principal would never notice as long as it was professional, attractive, and done on time. Then we could just switch to ants in the way our knowledge of emergent curriculum and our guts tell us to do!

> Teachers: We have a lot of knowledge and information that children want and need. But we can redirect our immediate plans and respond to children's emergent interests and conversations.

Do teachers have to let go of their carefully laid plans and drift in any direction suggested by children's comments and questions? Of course not. Teachers are still the authorities in the classroom. We have a lot of knowledge and information that children want and need. But we can redirect our immediate plans and respond to children's emergent interests and conversations. In the example above, the teacher had an outstanding emergent opportunity to initiate a valuable science investigation that children could learn from, involve their families in, write about, paint or sing about ("The ants go marching . . ."), and do research on: Are the ants in my house like the ants in the tree? How many kinds of ants are there? There are flying ants? Then there could be math investigations and charts about the number and kinds of ants. This kind of science curriculum is too rich in math, vocabulary, nature, art, and music to ignore just because the initial mission was to find leaves to press for a parents' night bulletin board.

If, when I was supervising student teachers, a teacher had approached me with her dilemma, I'd have said, "Wow, what a great emergent curriculum opportunity. I don't think anyone would expect you to do leaf tracings, but a great welcoming autumnal bulletin board in the front hall is still your responsibility." Yet frequently we avoid choosing our words as adults but interpret a suggestion as an expectation. Had the teacher told her principal that she had taken the children to the woods to collect leaves but that more important science curriculum had emerged and captured the children's interest, and she made the decision to follow the children's emergent curriculum ideas, I believe the principal would have thought, "Wow!" and been happy with whatever well-prepared bulletin board the teacher presented for parents' night!

Taking the Time to Develop Conversational Skills

We can find ways of addressing our concerns within the context of the children's interests and passions. Too often we allow ourselves to get caught in the pace of day-to-day life with children and not take the time to make interesting conversation with them or nurture it among them. We hurry from planned event to planned event without enough time to process what, why, or how we are doing what we do.

We have focused in earlier chapters on the effects of tone of voice and body language on our messages to children. Nowhere is this more noticeable than in the area of conversation. Children can tell when we are in a hurry. Developing strong conversational skills takes time. In addition to time, children need opportunities to think and ponder in order to learn. They need time to question and experiment. Yet frequently we prod children who are "doing nothing" into finding something constructive to do with themselves. Having thoughts, daydreaming, and pondering are constructive activities. We should provide opportunities for children to have chunks of time for solitude, self-talk, and just staring out the window!

Our observations of children should lead us to leave them alone now and again when we can see that they are deep in thought. It is always a balance. We want to encourage children to reflect, problem solve, and converse, yet we don't want to interrupt, coerce, or distract them. *Yankee Magazine* (Allen 2017) introduces award-winning photographer Barbara Peacock's new book *Hometown*. Her photographs capture thirty years of spontaneous photographs from the town she grew up in. One of these, titled *Snow Cones, 1983* comes with the following comment from Peacock: "I love how carefree [these kids] look. Even the boy in the back seems bored but he is still observing. Today those kids would be lost in their cellphones. I always think that people back then did a lot more daydreaming" (p. 113).

Alice Honig (2002) writes about the necessity of finding just the right tone of voice and thoughtful words to encourage a child to focus on problem solving without taking away her initiative. She also suggests that doing so poses an exhilarating challenge to early educators. I agree with Honig that choosing the right tone and words is an exciting challenge. In my experience, many teachers miss it because they are afraid to leave their own planning aside to get on board with spontaneous and interesting issues children present in their days with us. The demands of the future will not call on today's youngsters to remember information. Computers have memory. Children will need to be able to make sense of information, manipulate it, organize it, and understand it to be successful in the world they will inhabit. Meaningful conversation and problem solving, research, and questioning will prepare children for this task. As will, as Mel Allen's article above stated, daydreaming and reflection.

I observed an interesting conversation recently between a teacher and a small group of children. Initially the teacher was asking questions because she did not understand what a child was asking her.

- "Why were you outside?" Dante asked his teacher, Cindy.
- "Do you mean at outdoor play?" Cindy asked.
- "No! Why were you outside before?"

Dante came to this country when he was two. His mom still speaks very little English. Though he is learning quickly, many pieces of English still confuse him. This is true of most four-year-olds, but the language difference sometimes makes it even more confusing. It took Cindy a few minutes to register that Dante's question was one of these instances.

"Oh! You mean why was I not here yesterday?" Cindy asked.

Dante smiled and nodded.

"I went to help my mom yesterday."

"Why did he think you were outside?" Tanya asked.

"Because I wasn't here," Cindy said. "Dante knew I was someplace else, but he didn't know where I was and he wasn't quite sure how to ask the question."

"But if you weren't here yesterday, how could you have been outside?" Tanya pressed.

"Maybe because when I'm not in the room at school, I am sometimes out on the play yard," Cindy proposed. "Why did you ask if I was outside, Dante?"

"Not here," Dante said.

Tanya looked at Dante and then at Cindy. "I guess you're right!" she said.

Meaningful conversation can be a confusing thing for young children and, let's face it, for adults as well! They so often put a meaning on words or situations so much different from ours that it takes time and reflection to sort things through. Cindy made sense of a child's missing her and wondering where she was on a day when she had been absent. A less conscientious teacher, or one without early-childhood-specific education and credentials, might have dismissed this with "I wasn't outside," without getting to the meaning behind the child's words. Meaning is the key element when we have conversations with very young children. It is our responsibility to connect children's understanding of situations to the reality of that situation. The time to make this connection is frequently not available. Sometimes, though, if we articulated our concern to supervisors, we might get assistance from translators, native speakers, or the third-grade teacher whose classroom is next to ours who has supported the child's older sibling. But we need to ask!

The best way we can help children with this piece of development is by being meaning makers. Early on, I suggested that adults have a tendency to delight in the whimsical confusion of young children's experimentations with language. We chuckle. We repeat the stories. Sometimes we even write them down. But most of the time we do not clarify for children the error of their thought processes or provide more information that will help them come to more appropriate conclusions on their own. This clarification is essential to help children make sense of the world. Below is a story in which the adults were too slow to pick up on the meaning and ideas in a child's mind to clarify for him words adults were using to describe his new baby brother.

The mother of one of the children in our Head Start program was about to give birth. Her son talked a great deal about the new baby coming. His teacher had read all the appropriate books. Children in the class had talked to him about babies at their house. It was wonderful to see his very experienced teacher let the conversations fly about babies smelling poopy all the time, yelling too loudly, forcing the dog to stay on the porch, and not being able to play with you anyway "'cause all they do is sleep and cry!" His mom finally delivered an almost ten-pound infant. The size of the baby was the center of conversations at the program in the morning:

- "Wow, I heard he was huge!"
- "I don't think I know anyone who has had one that big!"
- "Colossal!"

I had the pleasure of lunching with the new big brother on the day his mom and new sibling came home from the hospital. I asked what he thought about all these exciting happenings at his house. "People kept saying he was huge. He fits in the apartment—no problem!" he said. It is clear that none of the adults had taken time to process with this little boy what ten pounds of new infant looks like. As I listened to him, I could tell the conversations he'd heard had him expecting something like Chuck E. Cheese or a huge float from a Macy's parade.

The thing that interested me most about this was that all the adults loved the story. They talked about how "cute" it was. Someone suggested sending it to *Reader's Digest*! Teachers laughed and laughed. Yet I never heard anyone say, "Wow, that's pretty scary. Can you imagine what he was thinking? It's too bad none of us thought to clarify things for him." I think this happens much more frequently than we might assume. I felt awkward that I had missed his anxiety and not taken time to discuss the confusion that sometimes happens between the way adults talk and the way children talk. Yet I was an administrator from the central office who was not part of his daily life at Head Start. In an ideal world, children would have teachers who know the difference between "huge" to an adult and "huge" to a child. In an ideal world, teachers of young children would know these things and act on them—not engage in giggling over the child's misunderstanding. These are the pieces of the puzzle we must make the general public aware of. Most adults have no idea of the differences between adult thinking and the thinking of young children. These are the things we must advocate for, individually and collectively.

After a fair amount of interaction and conversation throughout the early childhood and preschool years, the transition to elementary school is a bit of a shock for many families. Sometimes a parents' night at the beginning of the year and a few progress report meetings is all that can be offered during the elementary school years. Explaining to parents why you do what you do might be more helpful than (precious) time spent discussing how to send in lunch money or what time their children will have recess. My best suggestion for new teachers is to find a seasoned and well-loved faculty person and

Most of the time we do not clarify for children the error of their thought processes or provide more information that will help them come to more appropriate conclusions on their own.

ask how they manage the things you worry about. This is an intelligent and strong decision, not an indication of weakness.

The first step to doing a better job at conversing with children in a supportive way is to go back to our knowledge of child development and really think about the way a young child's thought processes are a work in progress. Reviewing the work of Jean Piaget might help with the developmental pieces. Or if that seems too arduous a task, find copies of Fred Gwynne's books *The King Who Rained* (1970) and *A Chocolate Moose for Dinner* (1976). Both are delightful reminders for grown-ups of how it sounds to a child when we say things like "Go to the fork in the road" or "Do you have a coat of arms?" or "We need more carpools in this community!" Another visual look at adult versus child understandings and conversations are the *Family Circus* comics by Bil Keane. One of my favorites shows a father and son walking in the snow. The snow comes up to the son's shoulders and the father's knees. The caption? You've probably guessed: "This is nothing! When I was your age we had snow that came right up to your shoulders!" As adults, it is true that we find these situations humorous, but as teachers of very young children, we need to remember that it is our job to urge children to question, explore, and find out. It is also our responsibility to gently lead them to correct information to replace their misinformation.

Here are some guidelines that will help you talk *with* children rather than *at* them:

- Remember that children don't like being interrupted any more than we do!
- Get a child's attention by getting down to her level, calling her by name, and softly touching an arm or face as you speak.
- Model pleasant conversation for and with children.
- Model appropriate differences of opinions (arguments) for children.

- Really listen to children. Stop what you're doing. Establish eye contact. Stay focused. Respond encouragingly.

Use expressions like these to encourage conversation:

- "That's interesting."
- "What happened next?"
- "How could that be?"
- "Does anybody else have an idea about that?"
- "Did that ever happen to anyone else?"

Make meals a place and time for conversation. Yes, manners are important, but it will take years for us to assist children in learning all the customs of class and culture. When a child shares an exciting story from her weekend with her mouth full, remember that encouraging conversation is just as valuable a goal as teaching manners. Encourage the conversation (see above) instead of saying, "Adelita, don't talk when your mouth is full."

Technology and Communication

Since the first publication of *Use Your Words*, the world and the way we live and interact in it have changed so dramatically that it seems another book is in order to address the effect technology has had on all of our lives, especially in regard to how we communicate. In the resources section, I make reference to the newly published and very relevant contributions of Drs. Patricia A. Cantor and Mary M. Cornish at Plymouth State University in New Hampshire in their 2017 text *Techwise Infant and Toddler Teachers: Making Sense of Screen Media for Children under 3*. In preparation of revising this book, I briefly did research to find what was available to help teachers and parents know what to do about the effects of screen media on children, language development, and how it affects their parenting and teaching; as is verified by Cantor and Cornish, the answer is not much.

I read articles that suggested the language skills of adolescents are declining as they continue to text and use media rather than having face-to-face communications with peers. I read articles referencing the longtime data focused on many years ago, the importance of facial expressions, body language, and tone of voice—all of which are irrelevant to today's tweeting and texting communications. When we attend the most recent of ECE conferences, we continually hear that relationships are the basis of everything in terms of learning. So how do we reconcile the contemporary patterns of tweeting and texting with the knowledge that human relationships are critical to language development and learning? The question sets many of us outside of our area of expertise. I offer a quote from researcher Michael Robb as it appears in Cantor and Cornish's 2017 book. In their outstanding text, they quote the following:

> Instead of focusing on whether young children are able to learn their ABCs from an app, we should be looking at what child development research has been telling us all along and asking whether the warm, language-rich interaction between young children and their caregivers that is so critical for developing the cognitive, social, emotional and linguistic skills children need for school and life success is happening when they use digital media. This exchange is where learning is most likely to occur. (p. 65)

Cantor and Cornish make the very strong point that the world has changed so much in the last twenty-five years that those working with children and families must increase their abilities in using technology. It is not that we need or want to have two-year-olds using tablets but that families are too stressed and busy for us to expect attendance at daytime meetings (when families are working) or to hope for attendance at evening meetings (when families are exhausted—and should be physically and mentally present to their little ones). These authors offer suggestions for communicating with families on a regular basis that are personal, practical, and online. For these reasons and others, rejecting the technological age is not a good move for those of us who want ongoing, meaningful relationships with families.

We have yet to learn many things about how to facilitate communication with both children and families in the twenty-first century. Remaining open to change, insisting that all of us need human connection, and reminding each other and all whose lives we touch that communication (especially in the earliest years) starts with relationships are some good principles to keep in our pockets.

In conclusion, when I attempted to close my updates by handing off to my colleagues Patricia Cantor and Mary Cornish, my editor called me on the move. She challenged me to make some final comments based on my four decades of working with children, families, and teachers. There is some collective wisdom there, she asserted. Two days later, June 8, 2017, my daily email newsletter inspiration arrived from ExchangeEveryDay. Deb Curtis, in her new book *Really Seeing Children*, shared a story that I'll paraphrase. She talked about a child approaching a teacher and asking if she was happy. The teacher, of course, responded, "Yes, I am happy." The child then, in language all of us who have worked with young children recognize, said, "Then you should tell your face that!" My four decades of work with young children and teachers tells me to encourage all of you to read Deb's book—and to smile! The children need our smiles. We need each other's. Like music, smiles have sometimes been referred to as a universal language. Choosing our words with care is good professional practice. Remembering that we are the grown-ups will help us on the hard days to keep in mind the children's need for our smiles. That way if we know it's not our best Monday, we can remind our face to put on its smile.

Discussion Questions

1. How can you handle children's developmentally appropriate yet seemingly random comments and interruptions in the middle of your group time or a focused discussion?

2. List some ways to have meaningful conversations with children at mealtimes.

3. How do culture, class, and other differences get in the way of children having rich conversations with one another and adults in their lives?

4. How does your program balance teaching children new to this country what they need to know here in the United States while learning from them about their previous home and routines?

5. How do you manage technology as a way to support families without letting it replace human relationships?

CHAPTER SIX

Contemporary Challenges

EVERY PROFESSION HAS ITS CHALLENGES. Usually trends in most fields come and go in cycles. Open Education is replaced by Back to Basics. We look to other countries, compare our test scores to previous decades, read up on recent studies. Currently research on early education is a hot topic. *Psychology Today*, the *New Yorker*, the *Atlantic*, and *Scientific American* have all had huge coverage, both positive and negative, within the past year or two on the state of America's youngest students and their teachers. Two consistent themes in most of these articles are the increasing pace of change and research and its stated outcomes. Many of these articles make the point that the pace at which we have new information often means that by the time a solid, well-done study reaches the general public (about fifteen to twenty years) and popular press, the premise has already been replaced in the research arena by something different or more valid.

Teachers, trying to do their best work, admit they have great difficulty keeping up. The word I hear most frequently is *stressed*. But the adjectives continue: *overwhelmed*, *exhausted*, *frustrated*, *discouraged*, *disillusioned*, and, from a few really honest types, *angry*. There seems to be consensus among early educators that children and their families deserve better. A few experienced and outspoken educators will add, "And so do we!" Talking to teachers has given me the idea that they are discouraged by developing competence at something that is supposed to help their children and then finding a year later that now research has informed us it wasn't such a good idea after all.

This chapter takes a look at some of the current challenges that make it practically impossible for teachers of very young children to (1) effectively do their jobs and (2) to experience true job satisfaction while working at their profession. Both of these criteria are essential to educating and nurturing a kind, enthusiastic, curious, and competent future generation. The Center for American Progress (Herzfeldt-Kamprath and Ullrich 2016), in an article titled "Examining Teacher Effectiveness between Preschool and Third Grade," had this to say: "Providing the necessary support for teachers to be effective is a crucial step in closing the persistent achievement gap and setting children on a path toward success." Most who study this area of research admit that it is difficult to pin down the details and even suggest plans or direction for what exactly is needed since there is not a national policy that governs education before kindergarten, and state policies (where they exist) differ greatly in expectations and outcomes. But the same article states, "While it is challenging to define a specific metric that captures the overall quality of a teacher, evidence suggests that certain factors may support effective teaching and ultimately produce better outcomes for children. These measurable factors include teachers' qualifications, namely their years of experience and educational background; the teaching environment, including characteristics of the school and teachers' compensation; as well as teachers' attitudes towards their profession, specifically job satisfaction and commitment to teaching."

Including here the reasons so many of our educators are truly discouraged and feel ineffective too many days of their academic year is also essential.

Areas of Challenge in ECE

As previously discussed, the web of complicated issues is difficult to untangle. But in an attempt to do just that, I have identified three issues that make it hard for today's early educators to effectively use their words with children—either to teach or to nurture relationships—*and* to go home at the end of the day, week, or academic year feeling good about what they do, why they do it, and what impact it has both professionally and personally.

TEACHER PREPARATION, PROFESSIONAL ADVANCEMENT, AND COMPENSATION

Doing an effective job seems less of an impossible dream to most early educators who have been well educated to do what they know is good for developing children. They know what to do. They know how to do it. It is the implementation stage where things break down. Why? Because in the United States of America, there is no sustainable financial source supporting the work they do. Quality materials cost money. Substitute teachers who provide coverage while ECE teachers attend important ongoing professional development activities cost money. Fresh fruit rather than sugar cookies for snack costs money. Thirty years ago, teachers often brought the fruit and the materials themselves, but since wages have remained static while costs and inflation have not, teachers often face a decision as to whether they can even afford to stay in their job, much less provide the food and materials for their classrooms.

Many of these teachers end up leaving the job with tears in their eyes. Why? They love working with children. They are good at it. They want to give back to the world. They spent years in college learning how to do the job well. But wages and benefits force them out of the field because normatively ECE does not offer a living wage, benefits, or a retirement package.

Then there are the child care teachers and providers who don't know as much about the field or don't have college or technical training. For these teachers, the wages aren't much worse than they would earn working at a fast-food restaurant or Walmart, but they figure the job will be easier and much more fun. Who can resist a freckle-faced four-year-old with a great grin, right?

These teachers who spend their days with young children have had very little preparation to do so. State requirements vary throughout the country. But when it comes to preschool, requirements are often as limited as criminal record checks, fingerprinting, and an interest in taking the job. Conventional wisdom holds that working with young children is fun and easy. The majority of early educators admit that the general public does not take their work seriously or understand how very important the work is. Many of the young people (described here as having little formal or even informal knowledge of the work) who take these positions show up their first day with that conventional wisdom in their pocket, a smile on their face, and an eagerness to spend fun and magical days with delightful little children who will laugh and play with them.

But the fact of the matter is that teachers must be appropriately prepared to deal with the challenges of this important, delightful, and yet difficult stage of development in order to educate children well. Without early-childhood-specific degrees and strong backgrounds in child growth and development, teachers will continue to fail in their best efforts to nurture and educate the next generation.

Indeed, without academic preparation, working with young children is very, very difficult almost all of the time. Disappointed and shocked, some of these young people don't last more than a few weeks on the job. Thus, the turnover rates in child care centers and preschools are very high. For our next generation, this truly poses a serious threat. Children need comfort levels consistently met and friendly familiar faces before they can learn anything at all. High turnover rates interfere with both social and emotional development and skill building. Low compensation and teacher preparation contribute to high turnover. So, no matter how well we know how to use our words, children will not hear them if they are scared, lonely, hungry, slow to warm up, or exposed to a revolving door of new teachers and caregivers.

In the February 2016 issue of the *Atlantic,* Georgia S. Thompson, director of the National Black Child Development Institute (NBCDI), discusses that teacher preparation and developmentally appropriate curriculum must be included in discussions of preschool suspensions right along with race and class. They are all "inextricably linked" to the crisis. Thompson states, "Young children learn through inquiry and discovery." She goes on to say that it is not developmentally appropriate to expect these little ones to sit for long periods of time. If teachers do not know or understand this, they are more likely to recommend suspension, expulsion, or other inappropriate interventions. Thus, teacher education and expulsion and suspension rates are closely related, though one might not initially make that connection.

The above article also links disruptive behavior to socioeconomic status and race. Thompson states, "Children in poverty often attend poorly resourced preschool programs with teachers ill-prepared to respond with appropriate behavior management." Though I agree that there is truth in this statement (many schools in low-income areas are substandard), it is also incomplete. Throughout the country, education levels of those who care for our youngest children are consistently lower than are necessary to give children a positive beginning in the education process. Lack of acknowledgment of this fact by both the general public and members of our own profession has always played into the complex mix of contributing factors. This includes programs in upper-middle-income towns and cities as well as inner-city neighborhoods. It is also a biased perspective to assume children from lower-income families are more likely to misbehave.

Also, to debate the issue of poor children receiving the least beneficial education, I respectfully disagree. Of the programs where ongoing education has always been beyond the norm, Head Start provides an outstanding example, yet the program serves some of our poorest children. The national legislative demand that 50 percent of lead teachers in Head Start classrooms hold a bachelor's degree puts those programs beyond the norm of typical programs (Mongeau 2013). Inconsistency in program quality and location is, quite sadly, the norm. Many years ago, Betty Caldwell, then president of NAEYC, said to me, "You know, the poorest children are getting quality—and the wealthiest! It's all the rest of us who struggle with this issue of access and affordability!"

Going hand in hand with the challenge of inconsistent preparation of early childhood educators is the equally documented and distressing pay issue for those who do this very important work.

In an *nprEd* article titled "It Doesn't Pay to be An Early-Childhood Teacher," Marcy Whitebook, director of the Center for the Study of Child Care Employment, is quoted as saying, "We have 20th century earnings for our 21st century hopes. . . . Right now if you graduate from college with a degree in early-childhood education, you have the lowest projected earnings of all college graduates. This is not a recruitment strategy" (Nadworny 2016).

Whitebook, who started her career as a preschool teacher, has been studying the low wages in the field for more than forty years. Depending on which study you read, currently between 45 and 50 percent of those working with young children have a college degree in ECE. Though the field can also boast committed professionals whose education level exceeds a PhD, as well as committed caregivers who love children, have no formal ECE education, and have spent their lives working for minimum wage or less to give children the best start they can, most of us would agree this lack of consistency, compensation, and commitment to children is unacceptable.

Though we have seen an increased interest in the past quarter of a century in terms of press coverage and advocacy, Whitebook's studies tell us that significant movement toward demands for appropriate training and compensation is very close to nonexistent. I am a third-generation educator in my family. My daughter is the fourth. So I have always collected profound quotes regarding teaching. In 1988, years before publication of the revised edition of this book, the Carnegie Foundation for the Advancement of Teaching published a report titled *An Imperiled Generation: Saving Urban Schools*. Addressing the many challenges still being discussed here in 2017, the report states specifically regarding teacher pay that "no other crisis—flood, a health epidemic, a garbage strike, or even snow removal—would be as calmly accepted without full-scale emergency intervention" (p. 32). Indeed, without a substantial and ongoing financial commitment to those who care for and educate America's children, ECE workers face an impossible task. Most ECE workers simply cannot stay well informed about current trends in ECE when they are too busy trying, as best they can, to care for and educate the next generation of Americans with what training they have and what energy they can bring to these low-paying jobs. It is hard to fight the good fight all day long when you also work at Walmart at night to earn gas money to drive to your minimum-wage job helping families.[*]

The time to acknowledge that we must change our approach is a necessary adaptation to that powerful statement from Marcy Whitebook that "we have 20th century earnings for our 21st century hopes" (Nadworny 2016). Yet we can't hope for those twenty-first-century earnings if we don't hold the degrees and professional standards that make appropriate funders take us seriously. Though clearly there is a problem with a system that assumes that the older the student is, the greater the expectation that the educator should have an advanced degree and receive better compensation, it isn't the only problem. It *is* inappropriate for those who have a CDA or an AA degree to expect the same compensation as a colleague who has an MS or MEd. Yet when this system began, the brain research studies that guide our work today didn't exist. We now know it is illogical to continue to place children at the most critical stage of cognitive and all other types of development in classrooms whose teachers have the lowest level of teacher training.

The existing model needs to be changed to reflect twenty-first-century knowledge. When Jack Shonkoff, MD, chaired the Committee on Integrating the Science of Child Development for the Institute of Medicine and the National Research Council, the committee's findings, *Neurons to Neighborhoods*, should have eliminated the idea that we can continue to accept the status quo for America's children (Shonkoff and Phillips 2002). Yet, nearly two decades later, the status quo carries on.

---

[*] The dismal wage/benefit situations described here do not include those pre-K and kindergarten teachers who are part of the public education system. Statistically, only a quarter of the nation's children are in public school early education, so the majority of our youngest children are in private sector programs where owners and nonprofits cannot possibly compete with the salary and benefits of public education—and don't.

Not that making a change of this magnitude would be easy. Indeed, an entire social and historical justification—that caring for and educating the young is women's work and as such is less deserving of worthy wages—would have to be overcome. Though a transitional plan would need to be put in place to alter the status quo at all, one of the most sensitive issues, at present, and existing for fifty years or more, is the displacement of hundreds and thousands of women who have accepted low wages and no benefits for generations to be there for the children. With good hearts and the greatest of intentions, they have attempted to care for and educate our youngest children to the very best of their ability. No one wants to diminish this work. But the world is rapidly changing. The needs, demands, and necessary outcomes are different than they were even twenty-five years ago. Our solutions must be different as well.

The 2002 book *From Neurons to Neighborhoods* mentioned above—written by a multidisciplinary team of scholars in neuroscience, developmental psychology, pediatrics, and economics whose mission is to bring sound and accurate science to bear on public decision making affecting the lives of young children—demanded investment and change (Shonkoff and Phillips 2002). Yet for the most part, children's lives remain unchanged in the necessary areas of nutrition, health care, safe neighborhoods, and appropriate education.

Beyond the issue of funders, the next generation needs and deserves teachers who have spent years both studying and reflecting on child development and appropriate curricula for very young children.

I'm going to share a related story of my own that I hope will offer solace to readers who are wincing while reading these pages. I told this story while giving a keynote address in my own state. It had to be in 2013 as that was the year *New Republic* gave extensive coverage to the story of four children in a Texas child care who died in a fire while their caregiver was out shopping at Target (Cohn 2013). It was a heartbreaking story. The provider was sentenced to eighty years in prison. It offered no consolation to most of us who believe a twenty-two-year-old should not have had seven infants and toddlers in her care. But that day of the keynote, many teachers were as upset about the "bad press" for the field as they were about the many other aspects of this tragedy. It came down to the age-old ECE dilemma of good child care professionals saying, "Now all of us without degrees will get lumped in with that terrible story." The providers needed to grieve and vent together.

One of our great ECE discussion points and myths is this: we want to think years of experience can surpass appropriate education levels. I remind people that you can have years of experience doing something poorly. This is not to say that the many fine teachers who have practiced in ECE for years without academic training are doing a poor job. It is admitting that children and the field need *both*. We need both appropriate academic preparation and years of experience to give the next generation what they truly deserve.

Without clear expectations, reasonable academic standards, professional codes of ethics, and a limit on who gets "grandmothered" in for how long, we cannot move forward to those twenty-first-century opportunities for all of our children.

ECOLOGICAL SYSTEM OF EARLY CHILDHOOD EDUCATION

Beyond their own professional training and abysmal wages, early childhood educators face other real stresses in the classroom. In the past decade, early educators have come under criticism for the outcomes of their work with children. Often the criticism is leveled by those who have no knowledge of either young children or early education. In particular, early childhood educators have been criticized for the following:

1. Sending preschoolers and kindergartners to public schools unprepared

   Frequently, this means the young children are expected to have acquired skills that are not appropriate for their ages. For instance, some primary schools expect kindergarten children to enter first grade able to read. Appropriate kindergarten programs nurture attitudes of eagerness and interest in reading but not the actual process of doing it. Sometimes it is the result of children never having access to preschool. This means that the critical skills of working as part of a group may not be in place. It means that some of the children do not yet know all of the alphabet, much less the sounds these letters make.

2. Allowing the seeds of delinquency to grow in our classrooms

As discussed in chapter 3, lack of knowledge of child development allows the general public to interpret typical behavior as misbehavior or even delinquency in young children. (Using the word *delinquent* when referring to a very young child is plain ridiculous.) Way too frequently, adults call *inconvenient* behavior *misbehavior*—something for which young children (toddlers through grade three) cannot continue to be suspended and expelled.

3. Implementing curriculum that is not developmentally appropriate in our classrooms

When this occurs, it is often the result of a few things: teachers having received inadequate ECE training; poorly planned district-level outcomes that require staff to ask young children to produce what they are not yet capable of; or the teacher's desire to give parents what they want for their child, even when the requested skills are too advanced for the child to achieve.

4. Teaching to learning guidelines aimed at elementary, not early childhood, skills at the expense of developmentally appropriate practice for both preschool and primary grade students

Many teachers are not given the choice of what curriculum they use; they are simply handed the curriculum and expected to implement it. Districts themselves often feel that their hands are tied in this area, as their funding is based on test scores or other exterior demands that put additional strain on both children and their teachers.

5. Doing a poor job of meeting the learning needs of non-English-speaking children

North American public schools do not have a history of requiring language learning beyond English. Many—probably most—of us are unilingual. We have no idea how to speak other languages. (High school Spanish does not make us bilingual teachers.) Yet many teachers in primary classes have more than six languages in their classrooms; non-English-speaking children are placed in primary classes within weeks of arrival, and neither the children nor the teachers know what to do. Teachers I speak with grieve this terrible situation.

6. Wasting time and energy on music and movement while other countries are preparing students to solve the problems of the future

Children need music and movement to find their souls and their way in life. Music and movement also give children an opportunity to exercise their bodies, an important part of childhood in general but especially so with today's focus on childhood obesity.

7. Being insensitive to parental wishes

As we welcome diversity, we encourage disagreement. Our job is to serve all the families in our program—from those who are staunch atheists to reborn Christians, from those who don't want us to ever even frown at their child to those who tell us it is stupid not to spank naughty children. We owe our respect and support to all of these families. We need to respectfully find policies, to the best of our abilities, that accommodate all of the families in our care. That means we have *many* policies, not "a" policy.

8. Being too sensitive to parental wishes

Teachers are often criticized for doing too much to meet the individual needs of families. Sometimes the criticism is from other program families. When a program develops a policy on birthdays, for example, that involves a circle of children making wishes for the birthday child but no cake or candy is involved, it is disappointing to families who want to bring cupcakes and favors. Yet it is unfair to allow clowns, balloons, and party favors for some children while some families do not have the economic resources to provide the same, some don't understand how birthdays are commonly celebrated in a country they may have lived in for just a few weeks, and some simply do not want birthdays celebrated at school. Holidays present a similar dilemma for teachers, who must somehow achieve a balance that satisfies families with opposing views and desires.

9. Not transitioning quickly enough from the demands of No Child Left Behind (NCLB) to the Every Student Succeeds Act (ESSA)

   Most teachers and programs have little power over their response to state or federal mandates. What's more, classroom teachers often do not even learn about new federal or state mandates regarding curriculum or classroom policy until months after the implementation demands because programs do not have paid time to come together to discuss these mandates. Families, too, have difficulty keeping up. Often, what they know about and want for their children are years behind the federal or state demands that teachers are trying to or are mandated to respond to.

10. Being indecisive about how children learn and what we should do about it

   Early educators want to do a good job for children and their families, but they cannot please all of the people all of the time. We need consensus and policies that can actually be implemented.

Unfortunately, early educators have often yielded to pressure to teach literacy, math, science, and even social skills—"please," "thank you,"

"I'm sorry"—in an artificial context that does not resonate with young children. Many early and primary educators have told me about the moral ambivalence they feel when they invest time and energy in a contrived approach to curriculum they are mandated to use by their district. They believe they have a professional obligation, using the best of their abilities, to execute the tasks their supervisors and district mandates require of them. They also feel, on a regular basis, that much of the push-down curriculum required by public and private schools does not appropriately meet the developmental needs of very young children. Many of them are tired of the demands placed on them to ask children to do tasks beyond their developmental abilities. They are also tired of the guilt and anger they take home to their own families caused by the moral ambivalence they feel about their work with young children, doing what blatantly defies what is known to be best for very young students. The toll, they tell me, falls not just on the children but also on them as professionals.

As an example, let's consider the stress level of a colleague of thirty-five years who is going on a trip to Italy after the school year ends. This woman, a graduate of two of our country's finest institutions of learning for early educators, is a friend, a mentor, and a passionate educator of young children. She has changed the lives of many families, has served as an American ambassador for education in both Russia and China. She loves children and education. I texted her last week and said simply, "You must be so excited about Italy!" Her response? "I am a classroom teacher. Kids are off the wall. District tests all this week. It's so unfair to the kids. State tests all next week. Same thing. I am excited about nothing!" My friend is not disinterested or clinically depressed. This is what our teachers are up against. It is unfair to the next generation and to our educators, but it is so challenging that no one really wants to talk about it, because what would we say?

Another colleague of only four or five years changed schools this year. She moved from the most challenging inner-city school in our district to the school with the best reputation in the city. We spent two years discussing her ambivalence about "abandoning" the inner-city school to take a position that might not be as emotionally demanding. She worried about the extent to which she brought home the pain, stress, and sadness of where she worked to her own young family. She has a graduate degree in ECE; in the beginning of her career, she was greeted by colleagues with comments about her "play" degree. Last year she had twenty-one five-year-olds, eleven of whom had IEPs. Seven were new to the city and the country and did not speak a word of English. I was able to observe her several times and could not imagine where her energy came from. She did an outstanding job, and those kids will all remember her kindness, her respect, her sense of humor, her face. Yet when the district handed in their numbers, some children in the classroom fell short. Those same numbers, however, did not disclose that the children new to the country had no interpreters. Nor did they disclose that the children with IEPs had no one-on-one assistance. "It shouldn't have to be this hard," this teacher said to me as tears welled up in her eyes. I encouraged her to care for herself and her family. The inner-city school will not be the same without her.

For a period of time, a television commercial for a travel agency featured a kindergarten teacher standing in a chaotic classroom surrounded by children on cell phones, children writing "butt" on the blackboard, a little boy sitting shoulder deep in a filled fish tank, a child duct taping another onto his chair, and children throwing things across the room. The teacher says, "All I care about is my vacation!" In the next shot, the teacher is getting a massage on the beach, telling viewers to check out the resort's website. I hope that my colleagues and the thousands of other preschool and primary teachers trying so hard to make order out of chaos in a job that is so critical yet that offers none of the typical rewards—reasonable pay, health care benefits, paid leave, and a retirement package—were spared viewing this demeaning, ignorant, and disrespectful commercial.

Its description does, however, offer a segue to a quick review of Bronfenbrenner's ecological systems theory (Bronfenbrenner 1979). Very simply, in this theory Bronfenbrenner suggests that everything in children's environments affects their development. This means not only their relationships (for example, family, friends, teachers, and neighbors) but also the totality of the influences in the world around them (government, media, school systems, community activities, community violence, books, music, films, entertainment, and so on). In the commercial that portrays teachers as powerless, uncaring, and ridiculous—a commercial that is played by major networks during hours when children are watching—we erode positive environments for children. We demoralize the very individuals who commit their professional lives to strengthening the environments that nurture and educate our next generation.

As we look at the multiple factors, many of which we discussed earlier in this book (poverty, equity, race, ethnicity, class) in relationship to methods of teaching as well as guiding children's behavior, we must heed the advice of Georgia S. Thompson (2016) from NBCDI that both teacher preparation and developmentally appropriate practice are inextricably linked to both the serious achievement gap and the preschool suspension and expulsion crisis. Though there has been enormous press coverage in recent years of both the achievement gap and preschool and primary-grade expulsion and suspension, the actual conditions of the individuals who do this work have in many, if not most, instances been missing from the discussion.

To move forward in our goals to improve teaching and caring methods in our schools and child care settings, we need to both acknowledge and take action to resolve all the issues and challenges presented throughout these pages.

We won't solve the achievement gap by hiring better reading teachers. Word walls and memorization of words, without a meaningful context, will not create a generation of stronger readers. Phonemic awareness, presented in workshops to caring individuals who like children but have no background in child growth and development, is as meaningless to adult learners as word walls are to three-year-olds.

As Richard Louv said many years ago in *Childhood's Future*, "Certainly a vast public effort, much of it by government, is needed. But the truth is that we need both public and private change. In pursuing this change, no one class should be targeted exclusively. Each family needs to reevaluate its own private values and recognize how those values shape part of the whole of childhood's future" (1992, 206).

Without commitment to a permanent funding source to provide quality environments, well-educated faculty, and continued support for teachers, children, and families, the American dream could become a nightmare. "Children are our future" is not a T-shirt slogan. It is *reality* for every country on the planet. The United States of America has the resources. It's time to invest them in future generations. As the many scholars quoted throughout this book have documented, it's up to us to make it happen.

REALITY (FOR REAL) VS. VIRTUAL REALITY

When we attempt to address the differences between virtual reality and reality, the rubber hits the road. In a *Scientific American* issue focused on "The Right Start: How to Fix Our Preschools," Deborah Stipek, a professor at Stanford University Graduate School of Education, states, "Until these funding and workforce problems are addressed, we can come up with the best teaching strategies in the world . . . but they are not going to be implemented" (Moyer 2017, 29). I agree with her. Right now it seems we have far more pressing challenges than what children are or are not learning in preschool.

In the same issue, Kathy Hirsch-Pasek, a psychologist at Temple University who studies how children learn, says, "We kind of forget that what's really important is raising humans" (Moyer 2017, 29). This is a piece of the puzzle that usually makes adults outside of the ECE profession (and often within the field as well) really uncomfortable. As parents, teachers, grandparents, and citizens, we truly do think and worry about the next generation, but often in a somewhat abstract way—and almost always in a very personal way. We don't want those "crazy liberals," those "rigid right-wingers," those "entitled welfare types," those "over educated academic types," those "freaky vegans who hate school lunch programs," or, even worse, the government to decide what it means to raise humans! Better to leave it abstract, right?

There is nothing abstract, however, about the ways that social media and technology are changing and have already changed the way we live:

- Research citing children's and adolescents' decreasing conversation and social skills are abundant.

- Thirty-two percent of children report feeling unimportant to parents who are distracted by their phones (Braff 2017).

- One in three parents say they have concerns or questions about their child's technology use in the last year (Pew Research Center 2015).

- Recent studies are daunting and revealing: relationships are no match for phones (ExchangeEveryDay 2017).

- "Our tools reflect the values of our time, so it's no coincidence that PowerPoint is a tool of choice in a world of snippets and sound bites" (Jackson 2008).

The *Wall Street Journal* commended Maggie Jackson in 2009 for concentrating our minds on a real problem to modern life. Her book *Distracted: The Erosion of Attention and the Coming Dark Age* (2008) cautioned us about allowing our ability to focus and attend carefully to be eroded by the cyber-centric, attention-deficit, overload lifestyles we all seem to engage in. Reflection, a slower pace, and capacity for deep attention, Jackson suggests, are the foundational blocks of intimacy, wisdom, and cultural progress. She discusses the fleeting nature of data, the false sense of connection created by hundreds of friends on Facebook, and the risk to relationships caused by eye contact being lost to the "eye, hand or ear on our gadgets, ever ready to tune into another channel of life" (p. 22). When *Distracted* was published, we had not yet heard of cyber-bullying or the depression even third graders feel when they read email descriptions of parties that they were not invited to. Jackson is bold with statements about our human purpose being to pay attention. Worlds ago that might have meant protecting one's family by paying attention to animal tracks or sounds. Today, she cautions us, "attention is central to creating a flourishing society built upon learning, contentment, caring, morality, reflection and spirit." Today *Distracted* seems so prophetic, Jackson's work should be required reading in college humanities courses.

A *Scientific American Mind* article about, ironically, good family relationships and intergenerational attachments, discussed the idea of "digital hypocrisy" (Sheikh 2017). I have always found it so much easier to see clearly the way my sibling, spouse, grown children, and friends could improve their lives and general operation on the planet while being blissfully ignorant of the enormous baggage I bring to the mix. Apparently current research indicates that the majority of us, as parents, suffer from this same malady. "To limit kids' screen time, try unplugging yourself," the article suggests.

The article also offers both surprising and scary statistics about parents' perceptions of their own use. Seventy-eight percent of parents surveyed believed they set a good example for their children as role models on how to use digital technology. Yet a survey of these 1,800 parents indicated that parents spend an average of nine hours and twenty-two minutes every day in front of various screens—including smartphones, tablets, computers, and televisions.

The article concludes that not only are children expressing that they feel the lack of attention when their parents' eyes are always checking the phone but also that they are learning to mimic their parents' behavior, choosing technology over human interaction. The article paraphrases Catherine Steiner-Adair, a clinical psychologist and author of *The Big Disconnect* (2013), saying, "Studies show that greater use of technology among tweens and teens correlates with shorter attention spans, a preference for digital time over physical activity and worse performance in school."

Of the many articles I have reviewed trying to sort through this challenge, most suggested a good start is making the dinner table a device-free zone. Relationships are built, values are shared, and ideas are floated in a safe space when families come together at the end of the day to share food and conversation. I am remembering, with a smile, a pledge that a dear friend of mine and I made in some distant city before leaving a NAEYC national conference. We were both extremely busy professional women with children and homes to run.

We agreed that we would put a tablecloth on the table and put our store-purchased supper into real dishes before we called the kids to dinner! The point is that it's not a matter of pizza or pancakes or pork chops—it's a matter that we all need to eat and, as we are increasingly discovering, talk face-to-face with each other. It's preferable for this research-based suggestion to be carried out while sitting down and that the time frame be a minimum of a half hour. Let's try it! Our future might depend on it—and future generations as well.

A Call to Action

Gloria Steinem (2006), social activist on so many issues for so many years, has said, "Change seems recognizable only after it's happened, like putting one's foot down for a familiar stair—and it isn't there." (*Doing Sixty and Seventy*, loc. 58/939 Kindle ed.) For many of us, some of the undeniable facts of twenty-first-century living have crept up on us in this manner. We didn't notice some of the very dramatic changes in our culture and our way of doing things until they were already a permanent fact of the way we live now. But with this recognition, we need to respond accordingly, and often this means adapting to the times.

For example, our textbooks and children's literature shouldn't depict all families as a mother and a father, two children, and a dog living in a single-family home in a small community. This has not been representative of normative American family life since the early 1980s—and was probably never truly representative of most families. Instead, we need stories that define families in the full diversity that exists today. This means story time includes books about grandparents raising the children, adventures of families with gay and lesbian parents, and portrayals of migrant farmworking families and children living in mobile homes and homeless shelters. All children deserve to see their families represented in books, on bulletin boards, and in classroom discussion. This will build a stronger future for all of our children.

Another perfect example of Steinem's idea that we don't notice change until it has already happened is the effect of smartphones and other technology on family life, education, relationships, and conversation. Most of the research I've discovered indicates that conversations and discussion within families and communities are disappearing! Let's set the technology aside in favor of meaningful conversation.

Finally, the changes that have happened in the field of early childhood education have led us into an era where our policies and practices need to catch up with the research and realities of today. So I offer these calls to action for all of us regarding the future of both language learning in a developmentally appropriate way and support for those who do this critically important work:

- Speak out at meetings, social events, or your state legislature.
- Quote Harvard's Center on the Developing Child.
- Access some of the resources offered here so you are well informed.
- If you are not a member of NEA or NAEYC, become one.
- Talk about turnover rates at administrative or board meetings.
- Remember that the "ecology" of ECE learning environments, politics, poverty, professional development, and worthy wages is woven into the challenge of behavior and achievement gaps.
- When advocating for all of the above, use current data (easily available online). Quote credible spokespersons (such as Jack Shonkoff, Jim Heckman, Erica Christakis, and Walter Gilliam) and *smile*. Complaining about working conditions, wages, and increasingly challenging behavior in children will not impress funders, legislators, or neighbors. Sincere discussion of what our youngest children need and how it could be achieved will.

Let's make a difference.

Suggested Readings and Resources

Suggested Readings

Barnett, Rosalind C., and Caryl Rivers. *Same Difference: How Gender Myths Are Hurting Our Relationships, Our Children, and Our Jobs*. New York: Basic Books. 2004.

Bateson, Mary Catherine. *Composing a Further Life: the Age of Active Wisdom*. New York: Alfred A. Knopf. 2010.

Bodrova, Elena, and Deborah J. Leong. *Tools of the Mind: The Vygotskian Approach to Early Childhood Education*. Englewood Cliffs, NJ: Merrill. 2007.

Cain, Susan. *Quiet: The Power of Introverts in a World That Can't Stop Talking*. New York: Broadway Paperbacks. 2013.

Cantor, Patricia, and Mary M. Cornish. *Techwise Infant and Toddler Teachers: Making Sense of Screen Media for Children under Age 3*. Charlotte, NC: Information Age Publishing. 2017.

Cazden, Courtney B., ed. *Language in Early Childhood Education*. Rev. ed. Washington, DC: National Association for the Education of Young Children. 1981.

Christakis, Erika. *The Importance of Being Little: What Preschoolers Really Need from Grownups*. New York: Viking. 2016.

Coles, Robert. *The Call of Stories: Teaching and the Moral Imagination*. Boston: Houghton Mifflin. 1989.

———. *The Spiritual Life of Children*. Boston: Houghton Mifflin. 1990.

Elkind, David. *Giants in the Nursery*. St. Paul, MN, Redleaf Press. 2015.

Falk, Debra. *Defending Childhood: Keeping the Promise of Early Education*. New York: Teachers College Press. 2013.

Galambos, Jeanette W. *A Guide to Discipline*. Washington, DC: National Association for the Education of Young Children. 1978.

Galinksy, Ellen. *Mind in the Making*. New York: William Morrow. 2010.

Goldstein, Dana. *The Teacher Wars: A History of America's Most Embattled Profession*. New York: Anchor Books. 2015.

Gramling, Michael. *The Great Disconnect in Early Childhood: What We Know vs. What We Do*. St. Paul, MN: Redleaf Press. 2015.

———. *The King Who Rained*. New York: Windmill. 1970.

Gwynne, Fred. *A Chocolate Moose for Dinner*. New York: Simon & Schuster. 1976.

Hayes, Christopher. *Twilight of the Elites: America after Meritocracy*. New York: Crown Publishers. 2012.

Housden, Roger. *Dropping the Struggle: Seven Ways to Love the Life You Have*. New York: New World Library. 2016.

Howe, Randy. *One Size Does Not Fit All: Diversity in the Classroom*. New York: Kaplan Publishing. 2010.

Hustad, Megan. "Up from Chaos." *Psychology Today*, April 2017.

Jacobson, Tamar. *"Don't Get So Upset!" Help Young Children Manage Their Feelings by Understanding Your Own*. St. Paul, MN: Redleaf Press. 2008.

Louv, Richard. *Last Child in the Woods: Saving Our Children from Nature-Deficit Disorder*. Chapel Hill, NC, Algonquin Books of Chapel Hill. 2005.

Louv, Richard. *The Nature Principle: Reconnecting with Life in a Virtual Age*. Chapel Hill, NC: Algonquin Books. 2012.

Mooney, Carol Garhart. *Theories of Attachment: an Introduction to Bowlby, Ainsworth, Gerber, Brazelton, Kennell, and Klaus*. St. Paul, MN: Redleaf Press. 2010.

———. *Theories of Childhood: An Introduction to Dewey, Montessori, Erikson, Piaget, and Vygotsky*. 2nd ed. St. Paul, MN: Redleaf Press. 2013.

———. *Theories of Practice: Raising the Standards of Early Childhood Education*. St. Paul, MN: Redleaf Press. 2014.

Nepo, Mark. *Seven Thousand Ways to Listen: Staying Close to What Is Sacred*. New York: Free Press. 2012.

Noddings, Nel. *Educating Moral People*. New York: Teachers College Press. 2002.

Payne, Ruby K., Philip DeVol, and Terie Dreussi Smith. *Bridges Out of Poverty*. Highlands, TX: Aha! Inc. 2009.

Plank, Emily. *Discovering the Culture of Childhood*. St. Paul, MN: Redleaf Press. 2016.

Putnam, Robert D. *Our Kids: The American Dream in Crisis*. New York: Simon & Schuster. 2015.

Rivers, Caryl, and Rosalind C. Barnett. *The Truth about Girls and Boys: Challenging Toxic Stereotypes about Our Children*. New York: Columbia University Press. 2011.

Roiphe, Katie. *In Praise of Messy Lives: Essays*. New York: Dial Press. 2012.

Schickedanz, Judith A. *Much More Than the ABCs: The Early Stages of Reading and Writing*. Washington, DC: National Association for the Education of Young Children. 1999.

Schulte, Brigid. *Overwhelmed: Work, Love, and Play When No One Has the Time*. New York: Sarah Crichton Books. 2014.

Senior, Jennifer. *All Joy and No Fun: The Paradox of Modern Parenthood*. New York: Ecco. 2014.

Smiley, Tavis, and Cornel West. *The Rich and the Rest of Us: A Poverty Manifesto*. Philadelphia: SmileyBooks. 2012.

Smith, Hedrick. *Who Stole the American Dream?* New York: Random House. 2012.

Solomon, Andrew. *Far from the Tree: Parents, Children and the Search for Identity*. New York: Scribner. 2012.

Sullivan, Debra Ren-Etta. *Cultivating the Genius of Black Children*. St. Paul, MN: Redleaf Press. 2016.

Szasz, Suzanne. *The Unspoken Language of Children*. New York: Norton. 1978.

Tyler, Anne. *Dinner at the Homesick Restaurant: A Novel*. New York: Ballantine Books. 2008.

Wiseman, Richard. *59 Seconds: Think a Little, Change a Lot*. London: Pan Books. 2015.

Woodruff, Lee. *Perfectly Imperfect: A Life in Progress*. New York: Random House. 2009.

Zavitkovsky, Docia, Katherine Read Baker, et al. *Listen to the Children*. Washington, DC: National Association for the Education of Young Children. 1986.

Zigler, Edward, Katherine Marslan, and Heather Lord. *The Tragedy of Childcare in America*. New Haven, CT and London: Yale University Press. 2009.

Resources for Parents and Teachers of Young Children

We are fortunate that the last twenty years have seen a huge increase in quality children's books (for all ages) that address some of the challenges discussed in this text. Because the Internet offers such a variety of easy-to-access lists, I hesitate to provide here what can be quickly and easily accessed online.

I offer a few reminders:

1. Teacher groups I work with often discuss this need. Many parents are so overwhelmed by the unforeseen and critical demands of being a dad or mom that it might not occur to them to look for support online. A brief list of web links on your parent bulletin boards and in cubbies and newsletters and online communications for your school families might be helpful. A school lending library helps.

2. Think quality but also individual differences when making recommendations. Topics of great interest to some families may bore or irritate others. Being inclusive and open to a variety of approaches is important in every area of our work.

3. Remind parents (as we remind each other) that "tender topics" books (as they are often called in textbooks) are an important part of sharing language with children for things like sadness, anger, jealousy, separation, and friendship. We don't want them pulled out only when a death in the family makes it a necessity.

Topics:

New baby	Life
Sibling rivalry	Nature
Differences	The environment
Anger	Fear
Sadness	Violence
Loss	Hurt feelings
Death	Kindness
Divorce	Manners
Separation	Forgiveness
Moving	Generosity

The following websites are helpful in finding information on all of the above.

California Department of Education. www.cde.ca.gov/sp/cd/re
/parentresources.asp.

Center on the Developing Child. Harvard University. https://developingchild.
harvard.edu.

Child Care Resources Inc.. www.childcareresourcesinc.org/publications
-and-multimedia/tip-sheets/tip-sheets-for-parents-and-families.

Early Childhood Today. Scholastic. http://teacher.scholastic.com/products
/ect/resources.htm.

The Family Conservancy. www.thefamilyconservancy.org.

Harris, Nadine Burke. How Childhood Trauma Affects Health Across a
Lifetime. September 2014. TED talk. www.ted.com/talks/nadine_burke
_harris_how_childhood_trauma_affects_health_across_a_lifetime.

National Association for the Education of Young Children. www.naeyc.org
/woyc/resources.

US Department of Health and Human Services. www.acf.hhs.gov/ohsepr
/children-and-families.

VROOM. www.joinvroom.org.

Zero to Three. www.zerotothree.org.

Links to Relevant Articles Regarding Children and Challenges Discussed in *Choosing Your Words*

30 MILLION WORD GAP: PROS AND CONS

Colker, Laura J. "The Word Gap: The Early Years Make the Difference."
NAEYC no. 3 (February/March 2014). www.naeyc.org/tyc
/article/the-word-gap.

Debunked! Unmasking Racism, Classism, and Sexism in Formal Education:
Ruby Payne, Deficit Thinking, Teach for America, "Grit," "No Excuses"
Practice, and the "Word Gap." https://deficitperspectivesdebunked
.wordpress.com/debunking-the-word-gap.

"Do Poor Children Hear 30 Million Fewer Words by Age 3." Skeptics. http://
skeptics.stackexchange.com/questions/20139/do-poor-children-hear
-30-million-fewer-words-by-age-3.

Hart, Betty, and Todd R. Risley. The Early Catastrophe: The 30 Million
Word Gap by Age 3. www.aft.org/sites/default/files/periodicals
/TheEarlyCatastrophe.pdf.

The 30 Million Word Gap—School Literacy and Culture at Rice University
http://literacy.rice.edu/thirty-million-word-gap.

"'Word Gap' Woes: At the Heart of Hart and Risley." Honeybee Connection.
www.honeybeeconnection.com/word-gap-woes-heart-hart-risley.

RACISM IN OUR SCHOOLS

Gilliam, Walter S., and Golan Shahar. "Preschool and Child Care Expulsion
and Suspension Rates and Predictors in One State." ResearchGate. July
2006.

Goldstein, Dana. "An Interview with Lisa Delpit on Educating 'Other People's
Children.'" N., March 19, 2012. www.thenation.com/article/interview
-lisa-delpit-educating-other-peoples-children.

Rowe, Claudia. "Race Dramatically Skews Discipline, Even In Elementary
School." *Seattle Times*. June 23, 2015. www.seattletimes.com/education
-lab/race-dramatically-skews-discipline-even-in-elementary-school.

Rudd, Thomas. "Racial Disproportionality in School Discipline: Implicit
Bias Is Heavily Implicated." Kirwin Institute for the Study of Race and
Ethnicity. Ohio State University. http://kirwaninstitute.osu.edu/racial
-disproportionality-in-school-discipline:-implicit-bias-is-heavily
-implicated.

Utt, Jamie. "10 Ways Well-Meaning White Teachers Bring Racism into Our
Schools." Everyday Feminism. August 26, 2015. http://everydayfeminism
.com/2015/08/10-ways-well-meaning-white-teachers-bring-racism-into
-our-schools.

POVERTY'S IMPACT ON YOUNG CHILDREN

Brooks-Gunn, Jeanne, and Greg J. Duncan. "The Effects of Poverty on Our
Children." The Future of Children 7, no. 2 (Summer/Fall 1997). www
.princeton.edu./futureofchildren/publications/docs/07_02_03.pdf.

Butler, Patrick. "In Their Own Words: Children's Experience Of Poverty In
Schools." The Guardian. October 29, 2014. www.theguardian.com
/society/patrick-butler-cuts-blog/2014/oct/29/childrens-commission
-experience-poverty-schools-in-their-own-words.

Jensen, Eric. "How Poverty Affects Behavior and Academic Performance."
ASCD. www.ascd.org/publications/books/109074/chapters/How-Poverty
-Affects-Behavior-and-Academic-Performance.aspx.

Why Schools Need to Be Trauma Informed. www.humanimpact.org
/wp-content/uploads/WhySchoolsNeedToBeTraumaInformed2.pdf.

CHANGING AMERICAN FAMILIES

"The American Family Today." Parenting in America, Pew Research Center. December 17, 2015. www.pewsocialtrends.org/2015/12/17/1-the -american-family-today.

Angier, Natalie. "The Changing American Family." *New York Times*. November 25, 2013. www.nytimes.com/2013/11/26/health/families .html?pagewanted=all&_r=0.

Craigie, Terry-Ann, Jeanne Brooks-Gunn, and Jane Waldfogel. "Family Structure, Family Stability, and Early Child Wellbeing." http://crcw .princeton.edu/workingpapers/WP10-14-FF.pdf.

Doing Better for Families. "Families Are Changing." OECD. 2011. www.oecd .org/els/soc/47701118.pdf.

Ivanova, Masha Y., and Allen C. Israel. "Family Stability as a Protective Factor against the Influences of Pessimistic Attributional Style on Depression." *Cognitive Therapy and Research* 29, no. 2 (April 2005): 243–51. http:// link.springer.com/article/10.1007/s10608-005-3167-0.

SCHOOL SUSPENSIONS

Neufeld, Sara. "Expelled In Preschool." *Never Too Early*. The Hechinger Report. February 22, 2015. http://hechingerreport.org/expelled -preschool.

"Standing Together against Suspension & Expulsion in Early Childhood." Back to Blog. NAEYC. Accessed December 5, 2017. www.naeyc.org /suspension-expulsion.

DEVELOPMENTALLY APPROPRIATE PRACTICE

Eckhoff, Angela. "Push Back on the Push Down." The Whole Child Blog. November 19, 2013. www.wholechildeducation.org/blog/push-back -on-the-push-down.

Is the "Push-Down" of Curriculum Harmful to Young Children? Illinois Early Learning Project. http://illinoisearlylearning.org/ask-dr-katz /question015.htm.

Willis, Scott. "Teaching Young Children: Educators Seek 'Developmental Appropriateness.'" ASCD., November 1993. www.ascd.org/publications /curriculum-update/nov1993/teaching-young-children.aspx.

TRAUMA-INFORMED PRACTICE IN EDUCATION

"Are You Trauma Informed?" ChildCareExchange.com. October 13, 2016. http://childcareexchange.com/eed/view/4243.

Evers, Tony. "Resources for Schools to Help Students Affected by Trauma Learn." Wisconsin Department of Public Instruction. Accessed December 5, 2017. www.traumainformedcareproject.org/resources/bibliography%20of%20.resources%20for%20schools%20to%20be%20trauma%20informed.PDF.

Rader, Jenn. "Using Trauma Informed Strategies to De-Escalate Classroom Conflict." James Morehouse Project. Accessed December 5, 2017. www.schoolhealthcenters.org/wp-content/uploads/2014/03/Trauma-Informed-Strategies-to-Deescalate-Classroom-Conflict.pdf.

MEDIA AND YOUNG CHILDREN

"Children and Media—Tips for Parents." American Academy of Pediatrics. Accessed December 5, 2017. www.aap.org/en-us/about-the-aap/aap-press-room/Pages/Children-And-Media-Tips-For-Parents.aspx.

Early Connections—Frequently Asked Questions. Early-connections-faq-102414.pdf. https://webcache.googleusercontent.com/search?q=cache:iYcjFIJjH2sJ. https://www.commonsensemedia.org/file/faq/download+&cd=1&hl=en&ct=clnk&gl=us.

"Here's Why Your Kids Should Skype (or Facetime)." Bloomwell.com. www.bloomwell.com/blog/heres-why-your-kids-should-skype-or-facetime.

Media and Children Communication Toolkit. American Academy of Pediatrics. www.aap.org/en-us/advocacy-and-policy/aap-health-initiatives/Pages/Media-and-Children.aspx.

Shapiro, Jordan. "The American Academy of Pediatrics Just Changed Their Guidelines on Kids and Screen Time." *Forbes*. September 30, 2015. www.forbes.com/sites/jordanshapiro/2015/09/30/the-american-academy-of-pediatrics-just-changed-their-guidelines-on-kids-and-screen-time/#3743553b137c.

"What You Need to Know about Babies, Toddlers and Screen Time." NPR. October 28, 2013. www.npr.org/sections/alltechconsidered/2013/10/29/228125739/what-to-know-about-babies-and-screen-time-kids-screens-electronics.

References

Allen, Mel. 2017. "Hometown | Westford, Massachusetts." *Yankee Magazine*, July 2017, p. 113.

Anthony, Michelle. 2017. "Language and Literacy Development in 3–5 Year Olds." Scholastic. http://www.scholastic.com/parents/resources /article/stages-milestones/language-and-literacy-development-3-5 -year-olds.

Braff, Danielle. 2017. "Your Smartphone May Be Ruining Your Relationships, Even When It's Off." *Chicago Tribune*, March 9, 2017. www.chicagotribune.com/lifestyles/sc-phone-relationship-family -0307-20170309-story.html.

Brice-Heath, Shirley, et al. 2015. "Invited Forum: Bridging the 'Language Gap.'" *Journal of Linguistic Anthropology* 25, no. 1: 66–86. https://doi .org/10.1111/jola.12071.

Bronfenbrenner, Urie. 1979. *The Ecology of Human Development: Experiments by Nature and Design*. Cambridge, MA: Harvard University Press.

Bronfenbrenner, Urie, and Julius Richmond. 2004. "Two Worlds of Childhood: U.S. and U.S.S.R.," *American Psychological Association*, 26. In an abstract of Urie Bronfenbrenner's 1970 publication.

Buechner, Frederick. 2007. *Secrets in the Dark: A Life in Sermons*. New York: HarperCollins.

Cantor, Patricia A., and Mary M. Cornish. 2017. *Techwise Infant and Toddler Teachers: Making Sense of Screen Media for Children under 3*. Charlotte, NC: Information Age Publishing.

Carnegie Foundation for the Advancement of Teaching. 1988. *An Imperiled Generation: Saving Urban Schools*. Princeton, NJ: Princeton University Press.

Carter, Margie, and Deb Curtis. 1994. *Training Teachers: A Harvest of Theory and Practice*. St. Paul, MN: Redleaf Press.

Cazden, Courtney B., ed. 1981. *Language in Early Childhood Education*. Rev. ed. Washington, DC: National Association for the Education of Young Children.

Christakis, Erika. 2016. *The Importance of Being Little: What Preschoolers Really Need from Grownups*. New York: Penguin.

Cohn, Jonathan. 2013. "The Hell of American Day Care." *New Republic*, April 14, 2013. https://newrepublic.com/article/112892/hell-american-day -care.

Curtis, Deb. 2017. "Really Seeing Children" in *ChildCareExchange*, June 8.

Dearden, R. F. 1984. *Theory and Practice in Education*. London: Routledge & Kegan Paul.

Delpit, Lisa. 1995. *Other People's Children: Cultural Conflict in the Classroom*. New York: New Press.

Dewey, John. 1897. "My Pedagogic Creed," *The School Journal* 54, no. 3: 77–80.

———. 1907. "The School and the Life of the Child," chapter 2 in *The School and Society*: 47–73. Chicago: University of Chicago Press.

ExchangeEveryDay. 2017. Early Childhood Email Newsletter.

Gajanan, Mahita. 2017. "Read Hasan Minhaj's Full Speech from the White House Correspondents' Dinner." May 1, 2017. http://time.com/4761644 /hasan-minhaj-white-house-correspondents-dinner-speech-transcript.

Galinksy, Ellen. 2010. *Mind in the Making: The Seven Essential Life Skills Every Child Needs*. New York: Harper.

Ginott, Haim. 1965. *Between Parent and Child: New Solutions to Old Problems*. New York: Avon.

Greenman, Jim. 1993. "Just Wondering: Building Wonder into the Environment," in *Places for Childhoods: Making Quality Happen in the Real World*. Redmond, WA: Child Care Information Exchange.

Gwynne, Fred. 1970. *The King Who Rained*. New York: Scholastic.

———. 1976. *A Chocolate Moose for Dinner*. New York: Scholastic.

Hart, Betty, and Todd R. Risley. 1995. *Meaningful Differences in the Everyday Experience of Young American Children*. Baltimore: Brookes.

Herzfeldt-Kamprath, Rachel, and Rebecca Ullrich. 2016. "Examining Teacher Effectiveness between Preschool and Third Grade." Center for American Progress, January 19, 2016. www.americanprogress.org/issues/early -childhood/reports/2016/01/19/128982/examining-teacher -effectiveness-between-preschool-and-third-grade.

Honig, Alice. 2002. *Secure Relationships: Nurturing Infant/Toddler Attachment in Early Care Settings*. Washington, DC: National Association for the Education of Young Children.

Hustad, Megan. 2017. "Up From Chaos." *Psychology Today*, April, pp. 73–79.

Jackson, Maggie. 2008. *Distracted: The Erosion of Attention and the Coming Dark Age*. Amherst, NY: Prometheus.

Katz, Lilian G. 1977. "What Is Basic for Young Children?" *Childhood Education* 54, no. 1: 16–19. A handout from a Lilian Katz personal presentation held in Concord, NH, in 1979.

Katz, Lilian G., and Sylvia C. Chard. 1989. *Engaging Children's Minds: The Project Approach*. Norwood, NJ: Ablex.

Louv, Richard. 1992. *Childhood's Future*. Boston: Houghton Mifflin.

McCartney, Kathleen. 1984. "Effect of Quality of Day Care Environment on Children's Language Development." *Developmental Psychology* 20, no. 2: 224–60.

Mongeau, Lillian. 2013. "Head Start Requirement Boosts College Degrees for Early Childhood Educators." EdSource. January 22. https://edsource .org/2013/head-start-requirement-boosts-college-degrees-for-early-childhood-educators/25375.

Morgan, Gwen. 2001. Personal communication.

Moyer, Melinda Wenner. 2017. "What Science Says about How to Get Preschool Right." *Scientific American*. March. www.scientificamerican .com/article/what-science-says-about-how-to-get-preschool-right.

Nadworny, Elissa. 2016. "It Doesn't Pay to Be an Early-Childhood Teacher." nprEd, June 14. www.npr.org/sections/ed/2016/06/14/481920837 /it-doesnt-pay-to-be-an-early-childhood-teacher.

New, Rebecca. 1999. Lecture: "Cultural Differences," September 1999. Presented to Strafford County Head Start. Farmington, NH.

Pew Research Center. 2015. "The American Family Today." PewResearchCenter.

Pope, Alexander. 1711. "An Essay on Criticism." *An Essay on Criticism*, 1st ed. https://books.google.com/books/about/An_Essay_on_Criticism. html?id=a0UmRwAACAAJ.

Putnam, Robert D. 2015. *Our Kids: The American Dream in Crisis*. New York: Simon & Schuster.

Sheikh, Knvul. 2017. "Digital Hypocrisy." *Scientific American*, March 1. www .scientificamerican.com/article/most-adults-spend-more-time-on-their -digital-devices-than-they-think.

Shonkoff, Jack P., and Deborah A. Phillips, eds. 2002. *From Neurons to Neighborhoods: The Science of Early Childhood Development*. Washington, DC: National Academy Press.

Smith, Mychal Denzel. 2014. "The School-to-Prison Pipeline Starts in Preschool." *The Nation*. March 28. www.thenation.com/article/school -prison-pipeline-starts-preschool.

Span, Paula. 2010. "Family Relations: An International Comparison." *The New Old Age* (blog). *New York Times*. July 30, 2010. https://newoldage. blogs.nytimes.com/2010/07/30/family-relations-a-worldwide- comparison.

Sparks, Sarah D. 2015. "Research on Quality of Conversation Holds Deeper Clues into Word Gap." *Education Week* 34, no. 28: 1, 11.

Steinem, Gloria. 2006. *Doing Sixty and Seventy*. New York: Open Road Integrated Media.

Stone, Jeannette. 2002. Personal communication.

Tanner, Laurel. 1997. *Dewey's Laboratory School: Lessons for Today*, 77–80. New York: Teachers College Press.

Thompson, Georgia S. 2016. "Why Are So Many Preschoolers Getting Suspended?" *Atlantic*. February.

Wardle, Francis. 1999. *Tomorrows Children: Meeting the Needs of Multiracial and Multiethnic Children at Home, in Early Childhood Programs, and at School*. Denver, CO: Center for the Study of Biracial Children.

Zavitkovsky, Docia, Katherine Read Baker, et al. 1986. *Listen to the Children*. Washington, DC: National Association for the Education of Young Children.